RE-INVENTING THE MEDIA

Re-Inventing the Media provides a highly original rethinking of media studies for the contemporary post-broadcast, post-analogue and post-mass-media era.

While media and cultural studies has made much of the changes to the media landscape that have come from digital technologies, these constitute only part of the transformations that have taken place in what amounts to a re-invention of the media over the last two decades.

Graeme Turner takes on the task of rethinking how media studies approaches the whole of the contemporary mediascape by focusing on three large, cross-platform and transnational themes: the decline of the mass media paradigm, the ongoing restructuring of the relations between the media and the state, and the structural and social consequences of celebrity culture.

By addressing the fact that the re-invention of the media is not simply a matter of globalising markets or the take-up of technological change, Turner is able to explore the more fundamental movements and widespread trends that have significantly influenced the character of what the contemporary media have become, how they are structured and how they are used.

Re-Inventing the Media is a must-read for both students and scholars of media, culture and communication studies.

Graeme Turner is Professor of Cultural Studies in the Centre for Critical and Cultural Studies at the University of Queensland. Among the leading figures within media and cultural studies, his most recent books include *Locating Television: Zones of Consumption* (2013) (with Anna Cristina Pertierra), and *Television Histories in Asia* (2015) (co-edited with Jinna Tay).

RE-INVENTING THE MEDIA

Graeme Turner

Taylor & Francis Group
LONDON AND NEW YORK

First published 2016
by Routledge
2 Park Square, Milton Park, Abingdon, Oxon OX14 4RN

and by Routledge
711 Third Avenue, New York, NY 10017

Routledge is an imprint of the Taylor & Francis Group, an informa business

© 2016 Graeme Turner

The right of Graeme Turner to be identified as author of this work has been asserted by him in accordance with sections 77 and 78 of the Copyright, Designs and Patents Act 1988.

All rights reserved. No part of this book may be reprinted or reproduced or utilised in any form or by any electronic, mechanical, or other means, now known or hereafter invented, including photocopying and recording, or in any information storage or retrieval system, without permission in writing from the publishers.

Trademark notice: Product or corporate names may be trademarks or registered trademarks, and are used only for identification and explanation without intent to infringe.

British Library Cataloguing in Publication Data
A catalogue record for this book is available from the British Library

Library of Congress Cataloging in Publication Data
Turner, Graeme.
Re-inventing the media / Graeme Turner.
pages cm
Includes bibliographical references and index.
1. Mass media--Study and teaching. 2. Mass media--Technological innovations.
3. Mass media policy. I. Title.
P91.3.T87 2016
302.23--dc23
2015012724

ISBN: 978-1-138-02025-2 (hbk)
ISBN: 978-1-138-02070-2 (pbk)
ISBN: 978-1-315-67520-6 (ebk)

Typeset in Bembo
by Taylor & Francis Books

For Jackson …

who says he might read this one.

CONTENTS

Acknowledgements	*viii*
Introduction: Re-inventing the media	1

PART I
Rethinking the media — 17

1 Rethinking media theory	19
2 Entertainment, information and the 'culture of search'	38

PART II
The media and the nation-state — 57

3 The media, the nation and globalisation	59
4 Rethinking media regulation	74

PART III
The consequences of celebrity — 91

5 The celebrification of the media	93
6 Intervening in the social: The function of celebrity culture	108
Conclusion: Teaching the re-invented media	124
Bibliography	*137*
Index	*146*

ACKNOWLEDGEMENTS

This book has benefited greatly from the many conversations I have had with other media scholars, colleagues and friends over the last few years. For their interest, conversations, advice, observations and occasional warnings, I want to thank Mark Andrejevic, Sarah Banet-Weiser, James Bennett, Frances Bonner, Charlotte Brunsdon, Nick Couldry, Michael Curtin, Michael Delli Carpini, Terry Flew, Gerard Goggin, Jonathan Gray, Melissa Gregg, Hari Harindranath, Tim Havens, James Hay, Andreas Hepp, Sukhmani Khorana, Marwan Kraidy, Tania Lewis, Amanda Lotz, David Marshall, Toby Miller, Meaghan Morris, Anna Pertierra, Jinna Tay, Anthea Taylor, Serra Tinic, Zala Volcic and Barbie Zelizer. My good friend and former colleague Mark Andrejevic has been particularly generous in reading draft material. I also want to thank those who commented on these ideas at the various conferences at which I presented papers: the ICA preconference on 'Globalisation and the Nation-State' in London in 2013, organised by Terry Flew; the 'Television in the 21st Century' conference at the University of Michigan in 2013, organised by Amanda Lotz; the 'What Is Television?' conference in Portland in 2012, organised by Janet Wasko; the second 'Celebrity Studies' conference held at Royal Holloway, University of London, in 2014, organised by James Bennett, Sean Redmond and Su Holmes; the ICA conferences in London and Seattle in 2013 and 2014 respectively; and the Society of Cinema and Media Studies conference in Seattle in 2014. I also pitched the book to a colloquium at the Annenberg School of Communication at the University of Pennsylvania in 2013, and benefited greatly from the discussion. The proposal for the book was the subject of a workshop during one of the Work in Progress sessions run by the Centre for Critical and Cultural Studies at the University of Queensland, and I want to thank all of my colleagues there who contributed to that discussion and thus to the book's development, but also for their contribution to making that Centre such a wonderful place to work for so many years.

This book draws on a long period of research on television and new media, involving several transnational and comparative research projects on which I was fortunate to work with some very talented, mostly early career, researchers, among them Jinna Tay, Anna Pertierra, Sukhmani Khorana, Zala Volcic, Mark Andrejevic and Adrian Athique. Given the international character of the research, it could not have been accomplished without the participation of researchers with the languages and cultural competencies for the research locations in Asia and Latin America. I learnt a great deal from them that I could not have learnt otherwise and I have benefited greatly from our collaborations. The interdisciplinary collaboration with my colleague Anna Pertierra, the co-author of *Locating Television*, has been especially rich and valuable. That collaboration continues as we work on further projects, but it has also played something of a role in the writing of this book; the benefit I have gained from learning how to see through Anna's eyes as well as mine is considerable and I am conscious of its influence even in a book that bears only my name.

Some of the material in this book has appeared in earlier and less elaborated versions and I wish to thank those who published these for the permission to make use of them here. Part of Chapter 5 was published in a less developed form in *Journalism* (Turner, 2014), and parts of Chapter 3 draw on elements of my chapter in Flew, Iosifidis and Steemers (2015) *Global Media and National Policies: The Return of the State* as well as a chapter in Volcic and Andrejevic's (2015) *Commercial Nationalism*.

The Centre for Critical and Cultural Studies has provided me with a congenial space to get on with my work since I stepped down as its Director in 2012, as well as the generous and impeccably efficient administrative support of Rebecca Ralph and Fergus Grealy. The Faculty of Humanities and Social Sciences has provided me with financial support for my research and travel. Working with my editor at Routledge, Natalie Foster, has, as always, been a pleasure. The two anonymous reviewers of the proposal made some excellent suggestions that have resulted in a significantly better book.

The final period of writing-up for this book was a little more awkward than usual as it coincided with my rupturing my Achilles tendon and being immobilised on the couch at home for much longer than I would have liked. The task of completing the manuscript, not to mention the rehabilitation process, could not have been possible without the love, care and patience of my wife, Chris, and it was made more entertaining by the companionship of my son, Jackson.

INTRODUCTION

Re-inventing the media

There was a time, and it is not so long ago, when those of us working in media, communications and cultural studies were confident that we knew what the media was: definitively, it was the mass media – broadcasting, newspapers and magazines, with sometimes advertising or the film industry included as well. There was no single dominant academic tradition devoted to understanding the mass media,[1] but within each of the approaches that were competing for dominance, there was a broad consensus on what the media did, and how we should investigate it. As Nick Couldry (2012: 12–14) has suggested, the main coordinates for these research fields were largely bedded down by the end of the 1980s: they were organised in various ways around the examination of industries, audiences and texts. In the critical media and cultural studies traditions within which I work, it was generally agreed that the cultural and political function of the media could be accessed productively at the level of representation: precisely because the media 'mediated' between competing interests and sources of power, the analysis of texts revealed the negotiations of meanings required. The relative simplicity of the considerations involved in determining what the mass media actually were at the time, and the fact that even the most commercial media outlet was nonetheless interested in creating and managing a public as well as a market, meant that the discussion of the cultural function of the media could be managed with the tools at hand – even though we may have continually argued about how we might do this, to what end, and what we might conclude.

Other traditions were equally well embedded within this theory universe, a universe that was, as I say, focused on understanding the mass media. Now, of course, it is what actually constitutes the media that has changed the most over recent years. In particular, the changes associated with the rise of digital media and Web 2.0 – 'connective' media, user-generated content, 'narrowcasting', for instance – have resulted in new modes of production, distribution and consumption that have been developed and operated in geographically, politically and culturally contingent ways. Among the most significant consequences of these changes is the fact that the 'massness' of the media is no longer necessarily the common element in the industries, practices and technologies we examine; social media are probably the most discussed instance of this. As a consequence, traditional theories of the mass media are no longer sufficient to enable us to fully understand the structure and function of what we now describe as the contemporary media.

I should emphasise that the changes in the contemporary mediascape I have in mind here are not simply to do with the new technologies in use, nor with the platforms through which they are accessed. While developments in these areas are certainly crucial in all kinds of ways, they are themselves subject to larger contextual (political, cultural, economic, historical) factors that overdetermine precisely how they are put to work in any one location. Furthermore, while the media remain central to the processes of modernisation wherever they occur, the character and direction of these processes vary widely around the globe. The precise social, cultural and political role played by the media in their various configurations in nationstates and geo-political regions around the world has become more diverse, and more historically and politically contingent. Indeed, as I have argued elsewhere (Turner, 2011a: 48), the less the media address a mass audience, the more responsive they become to the conjunctural conditions that frame their operations; along the way, they start to behave more like commercial enterprises than cultural institutions.

It is worth glossing at least some of the changes I am alluding to here to give a sense of what I have in mind. For a start, they include the varying structural and social role now played by national television systems in the post-broadcast area, the complex interplay between the global and the local within and between these national systems, and the diversity of the emerging patterns of localisation and indigenisation of transnational media trends, content and formats (Kraidy, 2014; Pertierra and Turner, 2013; Wilkins, Straubhaar and Kumar, 2014). They also include what has come to be known in many Western locations as the 'crisis in journalism' (Curran, 2010, 2011; McChesney, 2007), the proposition that the authority and legitimacy of the traditional liberal-democratic model of journalism is in decline, that this is partly due to the increasing competition from content sources outside the profession of journalism – from promotions and publicity professionals to 'citizen journalists' and bloggers – and that there are genuine questions about the commercial viability of traditional news providers within a competitive environment, right across the media, that is increasingly being shaped by the demand for entertainment.

In terms of the political provenance of the media, while once it might have been possible to assume (and I mean assume) a robust relationship between the aspiration towards modernization, a commercial media and a liberal-democratic polity, encouraging the view that there was a natural evolutionary path that led all modernizing nations towards a democratic mediasphere, what we now know about the varying roles played by the media in non-democratic and transitional nation-states, for instance, encourages scepticism about such a view (Mihelj, 2011; Sun and Zhao, 2009; Voltmer, 2013).

The development of the new digital platforms for the delivery and circulation of video content, the rise of social media (or what José van Dijck [2013] usefully renames 'connective media'), and the expansion in the use of mobile media devices, have created an extraordinary variety of changes to the patterns of production and consumption: the development of whole new media industries, on the one hand (Goggin and Hjorth, 2009), and the blurring of the distinction between mass communication and interpersonal communication, on the other (Madaniou and Miller, 2013). Media now not only create publics and address markets; they also generate and sustain social networks.

Finally, as many of the commercial strategies which enable these new modes of production and consumption differ significantly from those which underpinned the operation of the mainstream mass media, new business models have evolved. As online businesses discover the commercial value of the personal data they collect from their customers, a new domain of commercial monitoring, surveillance and data-mining has come into existence (Andrejevic, 2013; Turow, 2011). And so on: this list of changes is probably so familiar now to the likely readers of this book as to no longer require any further elaboration at this point.

While all of this has unfolded, much of the theory universe I described earlier as associated with simpler times still remains in place. Transformations and issues such as those just referred to above are certainly dealt with in the academic literature. Mostly, and necessarily in the first instance, they are dealt with in isolation – as intrinsically interesting developments that need to be understood in their own right. It is less common for the next step to be taken – a step towards the exploration of continuities as well as disruption – and this has limited our capacity to conceptualise just how thoroughly the media has been transformed. As each new element of today's mediascape has appeared, it has simply been bolted on as an additional component of what Couldry calls 'the media manifold' (Couldry, 2012: 17) without much in the way of an analysis of how that changes the structure, character and function of that media manifold.

Paradoxically, even in the most apocalyptic accounts of Web 2.0 (and there are a few of these!), while the projected practical implications of new media within their particular sphere of activity are held to be world-changing, their theoretical significance for our understanding of the function of the media more generally tends to be overlooked. Instead, it is common to find new media offered up as categoric displacements of what has gone before – a strategy exemplified, in my view, by the use of terms such as 'legacy' or 'heritage' media to denote television, radio and newspapers. While there is, then, a rich and strong literature on many of the issues nominated earlier, there is a tendency for these literatures to be disaggregated from each other, driven by relatively segmented interests and enthusiasms, more or less disinterested in continuities and commonalities, or insufficiently focused on the broadly structural character of the changes they explore. Consequently, there have been relatively few attempts to stand back and look at what the sum of these changes might amount to. Of course, I realise that this would be quite a task, so it is not surprising that so few have applied themselves to it. However, it does seem to me that we have reached the point where the sum total of these changes does amount to something like a re-invention of the media, and that our theoretical resources to deal with this – that is, traditional media theory plus the various bolted-on patches used to serially accommodate the next Big Thing – are, really, no longer fit for purpose.

It is true that some of these Big Things have generated their own Big Theories: foremost among these is the complex of approaches variously collected under the headings of new media, digital media and convergence culture. Elsewhere I have been critical of aspects of these approaches and in particular what most would now regard as their exaggerated claims for political significance (Turner, 2010, 2011b), so I should be very clear in stating that I have no doubt that the arrival of the digital – with the expansion of the online environment, the opening up of spectrum for broadcast television and radio, the development of mobile media and social media – has made consideration of these new territories a matter of some urgency. It is not at all surprising, nor, in the short term, concerning, that such considerations have dominated the treatment of the contemporary media environment for much of the last decade or so. Nonetheless, it is definitely time that these approaches re-engaged more comprehensively with the longer history of media studies, and with the full spectrum of recent industrial, political and cultural change of which new media is only one element – crucial and fundamentally important, of course, but not the only area requiring attention.

That said, this is not only a case of an area being, for a time, the focus of a disproportionate amount of the attention of researchers and theorists in media, cultural and communications studies. While, as I say, this does call for correction, and I intend this book to contribute to that enterprise, it is also true that much of what I want to discuss in this book will also inevitably involve the rise of digital media and their effect on the contemporary mediascape for all of us: consumers, producers, regulators, researchers and commentators. However, what also need to be corrected are the utopian claims that have been made for digital media's political and cultural effects, what I have called elsewhere 'digital optimism', which overstate the democratising potential of these technologies (Turner, 2010). This, in turn, is a product of 'digital exceptionalism': 'the idea that the internet is different from other forms of communication and therefore not bound by the same legal and market forces' (Marwick, 2013: 25). Alice Marwick acknowledges that, of course, 'internet communication has different properties than mass or face-to-face communication', but she is critical of the manner in which these differences have been 'extrapolated into a series of discredited claims: the internet cannot be regulated, it is intrinsically democratizing and so forth' (ibid.). While it is now quite clear that the utopian projections of the last decade were not warranted, as Marwick says, the vigorously partisan prosecution of these projections has been unproductive for the field: it skewed analysis and sent media and cultural studies sprinting up a blind alley for much of that time.

A key casualty of this was an orientation that had been fundamental to the analytic practice of media and cultural studies virtually from the beginning: a critical awareness of the market imperatives underlying the rationale for the operation of the commercial media, and a readiness to scrutinise the interests they served. One of the factors behind the enthusiasm invested in the projections that accompanied the growth of enterprises in the digital space was the degree to which media and cultural studies scholars uncritically accepted what we can now more confidently determine was in fact 'industry spin'. Jim McGuigan's (2009) description of the attitude taken by such scholars towards the digital media sphere, as 'cool capitalism', remains a telling criticism of the approach to that section of the media that involved the new media entrepreneurs. They became the acceptable face of capitalism in ways that newspaper or television proprietors had never been – and for no good reason. A number of writers have tracked the close cultural and historical relation between the Silicone Valley tech industry and San Francisco's counterculture (Isaacson, 2013; Marwick, 2013; Hillis, Petit and Jarrett, 2013), and it does seem implicated in the degree of tolerance shown to what Marwick describes as the Web 2.0 ideology, with its 'peculiar mix of entrepreneurial capitalism, technological determinism, and digital exceptionalism' (Marwick, 2013: 5). Of course, the reasons are no doubt deeper and wider than that, but a number of scholars, including myself (Turner, 2010), have drawn attention to what is, in principle, a fundamental error for those of us who work on the media: that is, giving too much credence to the media industry's own hype about itself. Nick Couldry has warned that 'media commentary about media is a poor guide to understanding what is going on in the media' (Couldry, 2012: viii), if for no other reason than that they have an immediate commercial interest in promoting their own products and a longer-term commercial interest in establishing their authority as commentators: 'media institutions' underlying interests in sustaining their position as a "central" social infrastructure', Couldry says, 'influence the accounts that media outlets give of the difference they make to social life'. To avoid the trap of swallowing media hype, he goes on, 'research must remain close to what people – all people, not just a technophiliac elite – are doing with media' (x).

I deal with many of these issues in what follows, but the simple point I want to make here is that although discussion of new media is the place where there has been the most sustained attention to the changing function of the media, such a focus on its own can still only address some elements of what matters about the re-invention of the media over the last two decades. In general, of course, this would be true of any account that focuses on just one medium or platform – no matter how convergent or dispersed. For a better overview of what the media does today we need to pull back a little, open the lens wider, and attempt to focus on some of the core, cross-cutting, aspects that exert an influence on what the media now does, in various ways, across platforms and individual mediums, but in most places for most of the time.

Where to start, with such an aspiration? I could approach the task one medium at a time, building a concordance of changes that might aggregate into the big picture I am trying to paint. However, since much of my criticism of the limitations of current accounts of the media is related to their piecemeal character, that would seem an illogical way to address the problem. Consequently, I have chosen a strategy that I think will enable me to address as much of the contemporary media environment as possible at one time. I have organised the book around three main themes – each of which reference both continuity and change, encompass all media platforms and formats, and acknowledge the diversity of media systems and environments across the globe. These themes respond to trends that are, in my opinion, of sufficient scale and significance to have shaped the character of what the contemporary media has become, how it is structured, and how it is used over the last two decades. They may not be the only trends one might want to chart. I am sure there could be other contenders, but they are the ones that have continually presented themselves to me in my research over the last decade. Let's see what their exploration ends up telling us.

The decline of the mass media paradigm

The first trend is what I want to describe as the decline of the 'mass media paradigm' (Hermes, 2013): that is, the reduced usefulness and applicability in the current conjuncture of a model of media analysis that was developed to deal with the mass media. While there are certainly locations where we are still dealing solely with a centrally organised one-to-many media system, they are becoming fewer in number and thus more anomalous. It is not, however, a simple matter of one paradigm giving way to another. As Couldry notes, it is the 'increasing interface between person to person media and what formerly were called "mass" media', that is the most 'radical change now under way' (Couldry, 2012: 2). In a shift nicely caught by Castells' phrase 'mass self-communication' (Castells, 2009), the take-up of social media has blurred the longstanding distinction between mass communication and interpersonal communication. Social media are notable for their hybridised patterns of use: they are used to build both personal networks and also, in some cases, a public. This mix of private and public visibility troubles the conventional definitions of what constitutes the mass media, and social media have also become one of the core sites for discussion of the proposition of a convergence culture (Jenkins, 2006).

There is more involved in the decline of the mass media paradigm than the rise of social media, however. Other developments which participate in the shift I am describing include what Milly Buonanno (2008) has influentially labelled as 'narrowcasting': this is the massive expansion in the provision of both broadcast and subscription-based television services which are aimed at narrowly defined niche- and taste-based markets. In many countries, the privatisation of public service television channels has contributed to this expansion, as part of a thorough-going commercialisation of both the broadcasting and the pay-TV sectors. As choices multiply, the mass audiences fragment; in turn, as competition for these audiences becomes more intense, entertainment programming is given a higher commercial priority than before. There are debates about the actual benefits of such a massive explosion of choice (Ellis, 2002), about the long-term viability of such narrowly defined markets (Lotz, 2014a), and about the fragmentation of audiences resulting in the fragmentation of a national public (Sunstein, 2009), but there is no doubt about the transnational scale and reach of this trend at this point in time.[2]

A great deal of debate has also been focused on the mixed fortunes of 'news' in this environment. On the one hand, the explosion in satellite and cable channels has dramatically increased the availability of TV news; in India alone, more than 100 24-hour news channels have been launched since the commercialisation of the sector (Khorana, 2012). On the other hand, in locations such as the US, the mass market for centralised broadcast news and newspapers has shrunk. Traditional news outlets have had to compete with each other ever more vigorously in their search for a share of that shrinking audience; at the same time, professional news journalism has also had to compete with alternative news providers across multiple platforms. This competition is not only commercial but even more crucially it is contesting professional journalism's cultural and political authority. The concept of the fourth estate is under significant attack in some markets – especially in the US – from a range of pro–am competitors, such as so-called 'citizen journalists', while news blogs routinely represent themselves as grassroots alternatives to the corporate production of the news – even though much of what the blogs circulate is derived from these corporate services. Typically, where the authority of the traditional journalism outlets is challenged, there is a corresponding decline in the privileging, and indeed the currency, of 'objective' information as against the promulgation of opinion (Andrejevic, 2013). This trend is reinforced by the commercial priority given to entertainment, encouraging the targeted hybridisation of news, opinion and entertainment values exemplified by Fox News. These shifts vary across markets, of course; for instance, while less than half the television audience in the US now tunes in to the evening news bulletins, in Australia the evening news routinely dominates the ratings figures – as it has since television began there – and television news has remained resilient in some northern European states (Curran, 2010: 468). Nonetheless, and notwithstanding their locatedness and contingency, these shifts contribute to at least the complication and in some cases the erosion of the expectation that the media any longer necessarily addresses a mass audience.

For younger consumers in particular, some research suggests, the consumption of news online is challenging the consumption of news from television and newspapers. While the websites of the mainstream media still attract the great majority of online news traffic (Curran, 2010), there is a growing (and interestingly, a transnational) audience for the distinctive mix of news available through, for instance, celebrity bloggers such as Matt Drudge, Guido Fawkes or Perez Hilton and online 'newspapers' such as *The Huffington Post*. If most of what appears through the blogosphere is simply remediated from other, more mainstream, sources, there are also new, independent, voices and new sources of information. Furthermore, online consumers are no longer constrained by the way in which news is presented to them by their providers; the capacity to personalise their news diet is clearly among the attractions of the online environment. Menus on the individual sites as well as news feeds through social networks, customise news to the preferences of the consumer. All of these capacities contribute to the increasing heterogeneity of the news diet the public, in many countries, now consumes.

Possibly the most significant long-term shift under this issue involves the reduced presence of what Daniel Dayan (2010: 66–67) describes as 'televisions of the centre'; the key component of these is the centrally funded public broadcaster. The twin neo-liberal policy imperatives of de-regulation and privatisation that have been so important in so many liberal-democratic states over the last two decades have motivated these states' disinvestment from public broadcasting. In Europe, in particular, where public broadcasting had been a central pillar of many of the various mass media systems, there was a dramatic withdrawal of state funding from broadcasting from the 1990s onwards. While there may be some indications of resistance to this trend that suggests the idea of public broadcasting remains relevant from the point of view of the public (Freedman, 2015), it is clear that any serious account of what has happened to the media, globally, since the 1990s, would have to acknowledge the widespread replacement of public service broadcasting addressing a citizenry, with privatised services addressing a market. Typically, this was accompanied by, or else responded to, the expansion in the range of choices provided to consumers by the commercial channels. As a result, users began paying for media services that had been, in effect, previously delivered free of charge, as a means of accessing this new world of expanded consumer choice. (So, for instance, there are many consumers paying a subscription for cable TV, but using it predominantly to watch free-to-air channels.) Typically, the expansion of choice was offered as a democratising force, enhancing consumer power, and as a positive alternative to the top-down, centre-to-periphery and one-to-many, media models that existed before. Here, too, as with narrowcasting and the explosion of news, the personal customisation of consumption is offered and received as a benefit. If the public broadcaster was at least partly about constructing a national community, the community constructed through the commercial outlets that have replaced it is personalised, rather than nationalised.

The media and the state

The second theme I wish to explore relates to the ongoing restructuring of the relations between the media and the state. The provocation to proposing this as a key area of change comes directly from the comparative transnational work I have done in recent years with Jinna Tay (Turner and Tay, 2009) and Anna Cristina Pertierra (Pertierra and Turner, 2013) which investigated the extent of the variations to this relationship outside the Anglophone West, but also from my interrogation of the claims for democratisation that are connected to such developments as the expansion of choice and access to, largely, entertainment (Turner, 2010). In some accounts of the relation between the media and the state, particularly those that deal with non-Western countries, there is a naïve equivalence constructed between the values of a liberal-democratic public sphere and processes of marketisation. The evidence is, however, that rather than the introduction of a marketised media leading inevitably towards the development of a liberal-democratic polity (which is what some of the accounts of the marketising Chinese media predicted) (Sun and Zhao, 2009), there is an insistent local or national specificity in the political arrangements reached between the media and the state in various contexts. Even as the processes and ideologies of modernisation and marketisation penetrate new domains, one has to be aware that these processes are managed by existing political, cultural and historical formations that are already in place, and they necessarily demand accommodation. Therefore, as the cases of both Singapore and the People's Republic of China demonstrate, even though it may appear that a more liberal media is emerging in the form of an expanded market for entertainment, this is not necessarily going to result in a more liberal polity in the broader sense. On the other hand, the relations between the nation-state and the media are especially important in the present conjuncture because of the media's close involvement with an accelerated trend towards the development of strategic national programmes of modernisation and globalisation that have become markers of progress, variously defined, within a wide range of political formations – including transitional democracies, non-democratic and authoritarian states, and marketising post-socialist and socialist nation-states (Curran, 2012; Kaneva, 2012; Mihelj, 2011; Voltmer, 2013).

I am of course aware of the residual orthodoxy in media and cultural studies, and within some of the discussions of globalisation, which proposes that the nation-state is now irrelevant to the operation of a globalising media. To some extent, this seems to me a product of what is now a receding tendency: the normatisation of the liberal-democratic model of the media that comes from a media studies that was overwhelmingly focused on the West and within that upon the global North. As the momentum of media studies' de-Westernisation increases, and there is now good evidence of this having an effect, that model of the media stands to lose its normativity. Along with it, should go the notion that the nation-state is no longer relevant for a contemporary media and cultural studies. Two transnational research projects in which I have been involved, and which ran over the last decade – involving research in China, Taiwan, Hong Kong, Singapore, India, Malaysia, Mexico and the Philippines – revealed (to me and my collaborators, at least) the implausibility of that orthodoxy as a general principle (Pertierra and Turner, 2013). Indeed, it is precisely as a result of the findings of these projects, findings which revealed just how crucial the specific contingencies of this relationship remain in each location, and how powerful and complex a role the state still played in many of these contexts, that my attention turned towards developing the analysis of the relation between the media and the nation-state as one of the key elements in this book.

The structural development of media systems has always been managed, to a greater or lesser extent, by the state, and there is also a close discursive and historical relationship between media development and national projects of modernisation. Media technologies – first, radio, then television, and now digital media – have always been deeply embedded in the various versions of modernity that nation-states have prosecuted. Within states that aspire towards modernity, the media is an especially crucial site for the unfolding of a narrative of national development and for setting in place the discursive frames for defining or 'branding' the nation.

However, the nature of that relationship can vary dramatically: consider the difference in the relationships likely to develop in, for instance, contexts where the state is strong and the media is relatively weak, such as China or Singapore, and contexts where the state is weak and the media is strong, such as Mexico or the Philippines. In the latter case, Jonathan Ong (2015) has argued that the commercial media has taken over roles that might elsewhere be performed by government in what he calls a 'television of intervention'. In a contemporary context within which the pressures of globalisation are forcing countries to engage with a wider economy than their own, modernisation is undertaken as an economic and a political necessity, but its implementation remains very much a cultural project. In developing countries, in particular, the pace at which modernisation tends to proceed now inevitably demands strategic management by government, and the media most often play a fundamental role in that process.

The crucial factor here is the market. As media systems commercialise, and as the processes of globalisation reinforce (perhaps even enforce!) that tendency, the principles of the market, and processes of marketisation, play more of a role. In some locations, such as the post-socialist countries emerging from the former Yugoslavia, marketisation is an explicit national objective, the subject of both economic and cultural policy – and in some cases it motivates a vigorous engagement in the project of nation-branding as a strategy towards more successfully competing in a global economy (Volcic and Andrejevic, 2011, forthcoming). In such a context, and indeed in many others, the operation of the market has become particularly crucial as a means of managing the relation between the media, the consumer and state-based processes of modernisation aimed at various outcomes – responding to the aspiration for enhanced consumer power, towards a more democratic polity, or the stable management of an emerging consumer class.

It is often assumed that the object of such processes, which liberalise both the media and the operation of the market, is the establishment of a liberal-democratic polity that would include, as a central component, a liberal-democratic model of the media. As Katrin Voltmer (2013) has shown us in her research on the media in transitional democracies, there is reason to be sceptical about this. While the liberal-democratic model of the media might be regarded as unproblematically desirable in the West, this is by no means a universal desire, nor a universal political objective. In authoritarian states, there is a tendency for a degree of liberalisation to be provided – enhancing the consumer's choice – but this is also a means of masking the lack of a parallel liberalisation of the distribution of political power. In such instances, the relation between the media and the state is aggressively and carefully managed by the state. Even when there is an intention to move towards the liberal-democratic model of the media, Voltmer demonstrates, the imposition of regulatory frameworks derived from such a model of the media is far from guaranteed to achieve such an outcome in every historical or cultural context. In the end, it is the historical, cultural and political specificity of this media–state relation which remains the most crucial factor and the reason why we need more transnational and comparative research outside the West and the global North.

The consequences of celebrity culture

My third theme focuses on the structural and social consequences of the pervasiveness of what has been called 'celebrity culture'. What I mean by 'celebrity culture' here is not only the body of images, representations, performances and so on devoted to celebrities, or the fan cultures around particular celebrities, or the proliferation of media locations through which celebrity is constructed and traded, or the industries that have developed around the promotion, management and exploitation of celebrity, but also the cultural framework of meanings within which the achievement of celebrity is assessed and valued.

At first glance, this theme may appear to be of a lower order of importance than the previous two; to some readers, I suspect, the media's contemporary investment in celebrity may seem merely to reflect a passing fashion in audience preferences. However, I want to argue that the establishment of celebrity culture not only affects the content, industrial practices and structure of all media forms, but that it also makes a significant intervention into the social – and does so particularly effectively across national and cultural borders. Indeed, in marketing, celebrity has become one of the most effective tools for the transnational expansion of a brand. The rise of celebrity culture constitutes a major shift in the social function of the media and it demands much more attention and research.

There has been a great deal of media speculation about this – much of it alarmist and uninformed – but there is also a significant body of research, primarily around reality TV, which suggests that celebrity culture may well have the capacity to influence or even to shape what constitutes an acceptable or desirable performance of personhood within our cultures. Discussion of what Couldry (2012) calls 'presencing' and David Marshall (2010) describes as the development of a 'presentational culture', suggests there is also reason to investigate the tendency, in some locations, towards linking the successful performance of the self with the maintenance of a persona online. There is certainly a sense in which there has been a 'domestication' of the practices used to produce celebrity online (Bennett, 2011) as ordinary people capitalise on the availability of the necessary digital tools in order to construct a public persona for themselves. Marshall (1997) and others such as Chris Rojek (2001) argue that celebrity culture is implicated in the desire for the construction of such a persona, as a means of simulating a version of fame, as well as in the establishment of the idea that the achievement of the visibility of celebrity might be a normal expectation to have from everyday life.

Such an expectation has met with considerable concern when it has been taken up outside the West (Kraidy, 2010). The global trade in reality TV formats, with their seductive deployment of the promise of celebrity and access to the 'media centre' (Couldry, 2003), has become a means of exporting particular models of personhood beyond their original social context – with the attendant possibility that this may contribute to shifts in the social context elsewhere. Fears of cultural colonisation, or of external threats to the maintenance of traditional values within independent national cultures, have motivated debates outside the West about the social consequences of the trade in global formats, and their disruption of the nation's internal management of competing versions of modernity.

While the nature of celebrity culture's intervention into the social needs much more research before we can make confident claims about it, it is abundantly clear that celebrity has had a major effect on the structure of the production industries. For example, celebrity content has become a major component of the news and changed the practices through which it is produced; the centrality of promotions and publicity professionals in feeding an increasingly time-poor journalism, and the creation of a newly corporatised paparazzi industry are just two elements worth mentioning here. There are similar claims to make about celebrity's influence on television formats such as reality TV and the reality TV/talent quest hybrid such as *Idol*, in which the emphasis is overwhelmingly upon the elevation of 'ordinary people' to media prominence. Most importantly, however, and unlike almost all of the emerging tendencies upon which the field has focused most recently – user-generated content, new applications for mobile technologies, for instance – this is a shift that is simply massive, almost universal, in scale. Celebrity culture is not only visible through micro-blogs or user-generated content on YouTube, but it also generates core content for mainstream newspapers, primetime television, talk radio and the websites for just about every news and entertainment outlet in the business, as well as driving the dominant television formats that are currently traded around the globe. This is no mere niche interest of the early adopters; this is fundamental to what the mass media, and increasingly social media, do today. That said, it is important to acknowledge that what celebrity culture does, of course, it does not do on its own; in most cases, celebrity culture has acted in concert with, for instance, forces of commercialisation and the associated rise in the privileging of entertainment content over information (in newspapers, on their websites as well as in print). So, there is still a lot of work to do in this area before we fully understand the manner in which celebrity culture has played its role in the re-invention of the media.

This book is organised in three parts, each of which develop aspects of the three themes outlined above. Part I is called 'Rethinking the Media', and it addresses, in several ways, some of theoretical issues that are raised for media studies by the re-invention of the media. Chapter 1, 'Rethinking media theory', responds to the decline of the mass media paradigm by investigating how we might rethink our approaches to the media to properly accommodate this shift. After reviewing the benefits and limits of theories of convergence and of mediatisation, the chapter concludes by asking whether media and cultural studies' approaches to the contemporary media have paid enough attention to the media's commercialisation and its influence on the interests now served by the deployment of media power. Chapter 2, 'Entertainment, information and "the culture of search"', takes the media's commercialisation as its starting point by examining one of its key effects – the prioritisation of entertainment content over information. The initial focus is upon the news media's gradual reorientation around the provision of entertainment, and how that has affected the definition, status and authority of news. The chapter then locates that reorientation in a context where consumers' access to information online has massively expanded – a development which might be seen to constitute a significantly countervailing and positive force. As what Hillis *et al.* (2013) describe as 'the culture of search' has become increasingly embedded in the practices of everyday life, there is now a significant debate about just how 'empowering' this enhanced access to information has turned out to be, and for whom. Part II is entitled 'The Media and the Nation-State', and Chapter 3, 'The media, the nation and globalisation', responds to what I suggest is a relatively recent shift in the orthodox attitude within media and cultural studies to the contemporary relevance of the nation-state. There is an emerging understanding, the chapter argues, of the need to recognise and to investigate the diversity of media systems around the world; paramount among the contexts for such an investigation are the operating environments established by the nation-state – environments that are marked by their political, historical and cultural contingency. Drawing in particular on the growing body of transnational and comparative research from outside the West, as well as a body of original research in Asia and Latin America, the chapter argues for the importance of detailed and located attention to these environments, and in particular to the role played by processes of modernisation, if we are to improve our understanding of the ways in which relationships between the media and the nation-state are being reconfigured currently around the globe. Chapter 4, 'Rethinking media regulation', acknowledges the scale of the challenge facing those who wish to regulate the re-invented media, as the pace of change has outstripped the capacity of policy to respond – and, even more importantly, as governments have been increasingly inclined to abandon this sphere of interest to the workings of the market. Nonetheless, despite its currently unfashionable status, regulation will continue to be an issue as long as we see the media as constituting a fundamental component of the public sphere within a democratic polity. This chapter makes a case for some reinvestment in that principle, and for taking the task of rethinking media regulation seriously once more: to revive the political will required to devise contemporary regulatory strategies aimed at ensuring that the media operate not only in their own interests, but also in the interest of the public. It considers this principle in relation to two areas: the protection of privacy online and the support for a journalism aimed at the public good, rather than merely commercial survival. Finally, the chapter discusses some of the implications for a liberal-democratic regulatory regime that emerge from Katrin Voltmer's (2013) recent work on media regulation within transitional democracies.

The chapters in Part III, 'The Consequences of Celebrity', address two central issues that I argue need to be framed as among the consequences of the rise of celebrity culture. Chapter 5, 'The celebrification of the media', puts flesh on the bones of my claim that celebrity has changed the industrial structure of the media and their production practices by looking at celebrity's effect on the production of news. The chapter outlines what is distinctive about the newsgathering practices that have developed in relation to the establishment and expansion of celebrity news. These include how celebrity news has developed in tandem with the integration of the publicity and promotions industries into the mainstream of media production, the increasing importance of the visual in celebrity news with the corresponding incorporation of the paparazzi into the standard processes for the production of news, and the extension of the journalistic provenance of gossip. Not only are these shifts significant in themselves, but some of these practices also involve quite significant departures from traditional journalistic principles, and thus carry implications for the wider enterprise of journalism, and for its social function. Chapter 6, 'Intervening in the social: The function of celebrity culture', takes on what is becoming an important question for those who have begun to consider the possible cultural and social consequences of celebrity: the role that celebrity culture plays in everyday life. While there are regular bouts of public debate about the likely social impact of the values, discourses and behaviours that are popularised by celebrities and their media vehicles such as reality TV programmes, there is conflicting evidence about precisely how celebrity culture might play a role that extends beyond our consumption of media texts into the wider domain of the social. Some research suggests that celebrity culture is a powerful and culturally pervasive discursive influence, successfully modelling new ways of performing 'personhood' (Marshall, 2010), while others argue for a more politically nuanced explanation of how celebrity might 'intervene in the social' (Bratich, 2007). The two arenas of debate examined in this chapter concern the performance of the 'ordinary celebrity' on reality TV, and the construction of a persona for the micro-celebrity online.

Finally, the concluding chapter, 'Teaching the re-invented media', sets out to do two things. First, it presents a summary of what emerge from the preceding chapters as the core components of the re-invented media, and considers their implications. Second, it responds to the question of how we should go about teaching this version of the media. The reason why this latter issue is a particularly urgent question is that the curriculum for media studies has been gradually dividing itself into two, potentially exclusive, sets of interests. As programmes in digital media, new media studies and the like develop, they are increasingly doing so in isolation from the histories and concerns of traditional media studies, and indeed of traditional media. While understandable in principle – those working on these fields are perfectly entitled to develop this as a discrete area of interest – it does not help us towards the objective of finding an inclusive and comprehensive framework within which to place the study and analysis of the contemporary media. Not only are we dealing with a media studies that has yet to thoroughly renovate its view of the media in order to incorporate the dramatic changes that have provoked the approach taken in this book, but we are now seeing the evolution of new formations of the curriculum which threaten to institutionalise the partiality of that vision. I don't think this serves us well. I conclude the chapter, and the book, by offering some opinions about the dangers and the inadequacies of the divided curriculum at the present time, before going on to make some positive suggestions about what the curriculum for a more inclusive media studies – that is, a media studies that is interested in working with the *whole* of the re-invented media – might look like.

Notes

1 To be clear, the context from which I am writing is one in which media studies, communications studies and cultural studies would all regard themselves as contributing to the understanding of the mass media in various ways. In particular national contexts, one or other of these traditions might be institutionally dominant – communications studies is the dominant field in the US, for instance – as their influence does vary considerably across national academic traditions. However, I am also aware of disciplines such as cultural anthropology taking the lead in the study of the media elsewhere, such as in some Latin American contexts. The comments I am making here refer to the traditions I know best – those of Anglophone media, communications and cultural studies.
2 It is probably worth noting, however, that the development of online TV services such as Apple TV, with their relatively restricted menu of channels, constitutes a significant reversal of the long-running trend towards the 500-channel universe.

PART I
Rethinking the media

1
RETHINKING MEDIA THEORY

This first chapter addresses the question of how we might begin to rethink media theory in the light of the decline of the mass media paradigm. It does this by examining two important directions within the discussion of the contemporary media, before returning to a question that, in my view, has tended to be put on the backburner as a result of the political optimism that has coloured the digital era – the analysis of media power. First, I consider the usefulness, in this context, of theories built around the concept of media convergence, something that has occupied a great deal of media and cultural studies thinking about new and connective media over the last decade. Second, the chapter looks more briefly at theories of mediatisation as a means of providing a more comprehensive overview of the contemporary media that extends the focus of media theory beyond the consideration of new media and the digital. Third, and in some ways extending the critique of 'digital optimism' I have developed in previous work (Turner, 2010), this chapter asks how we might reconfigure theories of media power in the current conjuncture. Finally, and this is a theme that informs the arguments throughout this chapter, I question whether media and cultural studies have sufficiently confronted the implications of the increasing commercialisation of the media, and its effect on the character of the interests served by the deployment of the media's symbolic power.

In many locations today, it is possible to argue that we have moved from living in a 'mass-mediated' to a 'multi-mediated' culture (Couldry, Livingstone and Markham, 2010: 35). Whole sectors of the media no longer address us as a mass audience, as the way that the media industries now think of their audiences is significantly changing. Without necessarily completely abandoning their earlier business models, in which they gathered mass audiences to sell to advertisers, media industries have also had to develop new ways of tracking, targeting and attracting much thinner slices of the population. These slices are defined by, and accumulate their commercial value through, their patterns of consumption. In a cruel inversion of the politics of Jay Rosen's (2006) utopian manifesto for audience empowerment, it seems as if 'consumers' is now the most applicable label for 'the people formerly known as the audience'.

As Joseph Turow argues in *The Daily You* (Turow, 2011), this tendency is not confined to the media, as only attributable to the changing affordances of media technologies, for instance, but rather it is embedded within larger societal, political and economic shifts as well – such as those elements of what is often called neoliberalism which have successfully built the discursive connection between consumerism and citizenship. In her analysis of 21st century brand culture within the US, Sarah Banet-Weiser argues that, in 'advanced capitalism, connections between consumerism and citizenship' no longer need to be 'justified or qualified':

> In the era of mass consumption, such connections had to be sold by advertisers (so that buying a product was crafted as a choice afforded by democratic freedoms); in the 1970s and 1980s such connections had to be justified by market segmentation (as identities became products like any other material good, marketers could naturalize the position of politics with commercialism, or citizenship with consumption, as a relationship). However, the consumer citizen *is* the central category of analysis for today's advanced capitalist culture. Individual freedoms are guaranteed not by the state or another institution but by the freedom of the market and of trade. (Banet-Weiser, 2012: 44)

Banet-Weiser goes on to suggest that the emphasis on the 'mass' she identifies in the era of mass consumption and production, as well as the focus upon identity groups within the niche market era (what she describes above as market segmentation), have, in the contemporary era, been 'redefined as an emphasis on "the particular"'(ibid.).

Of course, and while Banet-Weiser's analysis would certainly resonate across most Western democracies, there could be a quite different narrative of change in other locations – where there are different social and economic histories, or where capitalism's influence is mediated by other political forces, for instance. The heterogeneity and diversity of media experiences around the globe has increased at the same time as the pace of technological and structural change has accelerated. There is reason to see a connection, as I have noted earlier: to suggest that, 'as mass media lose their massness, they become much more conjunctural, much more volatile and contingent in response to the precise configuration of the forces of change in particular social–historical circumstances' (Turner, 2011a: 48). Given this volatility and its varied outcomes, the traditional paradigms for the analysis of the mass media require reassessment if media and cultural studies are to better understand the altered states of the media today, and to find ways of mapping their coordinates.

While there has been a massive expansion in media provision and consumer choice, globally, and while there is also evidence that in some markets the audience for the mass media is shrinking, the current conjuncture does not simply present us with a straightforward scenario of multiplying choices, fragmenting audiences and a growing engagement with the application of new media technologies. It is more complicated than that – and, indeed, it has played out in ways many did not expect. For a start, despite predictions that Web 2.0 would transfer some of the power held by the mainstream media into the hands of the audience (Rosen, 2006) or to the so-called 'produsers' (Bruns, 2008), it now appears that what we might call Big Media have gradually colonised the online environment, creating what Napoli, with some prescience, described as 'the massification' of the internet (Napoli, 2008: 60). Geert Lovink, among others, has lamented the fact that 'in most countries' today, the new media spaces are 'owned by literally three or four companies', giving them 'phenomenal power to shape the architecture of such interactions' (Lovink, 2013:10). Among the first to recognise the progressive political potential of the Web, but also among the first to warn against that potential being squandered, Lovink is clearly frustrated by this situation: 'whereas the hegemonic internet ideology promises open, decentralised systems, why do we, time and again, find ourselves locked into closed, centralised environments? Why are individual users so easily lured into these corporate "walled gardens"?' (10), he asks. For Lovink, in this latest book (Lovink and Rasch, 2013), the most important questions to be raised about social media today are not about the politics of user empowerment, but about the political economy of social media monopolies (11).

José van Dijck's account of the history of YouTube suggests that it was probably never going to be otherwise, given the long history of the trends towards 'personalization, mass customization, commercialization, and the blending of public and private space' that preceded the current configurations, as well as the persistent encroachment of the market into 'the culture of connectivity':

> [I]t is easy to understand why YouTube's alternative image, which thrived on a cultural mood of participation and community building, could never hold up in the face of the powerful commercial incentives propelling the site into the mainstream. The neoliberal ideology of technology pushing economic needs is not always conducive to the ideal of creating a sustainable environment that nourishes community-based platforms. Commercial owners favour – over the need for sustainable communities – quick turnovers, short-lived trends, celebrities attracting mass audiences, attention-grabbing experiences, influential power-users, and a large pool of aspiring professionals. (van Dijck, 2013: 130)

As van Dijck points out, even as the operation of this commercial logic actually pushed the platform 'back the other way from connectedness' (131), it is 'remarkable how often the participatory ideal of connectedness is invoked to warrant the needs for commercial exploitation of connectivity' (130). Notwithstanding its continuing invocation, YouTube's embodiment of this ideal is looking increasingly threadbare: most of its menu is derived from television in the first place, the material uploaded is mostly 'user-copied' rather than 'user-generated', and it has moved away from being structured like an open database towards something that is becoming more like a multi-channel television network (119).

There is also the fact that the politics underlying the performance of participatory culture can turn out to be deeply conflicted. Banet-Weiser has discussed the contradictions embedded in, soap and cosmetics manufacturer, Dove's interactive Campaign for Real Beauty. On the one hand, she says, Dove's beauty products are 'created for women and girls to more closely approximate a feminine ideal', that is, on the other hand, made the object of critique through the Campaign for Real Beauty's promotion of a 'wider definition of beauty' (that is, less idealised and more 'truthful') and through its invitations for consumer participation in the production of that critique (Banet-Weiser, 2012: 41). Banet-Weiser shows how successfully these contradictions are managed, rather than reconciled, as the Dove campaign relays 'feminist critiques of the beauty industry while at the same time deflecting those same critiques from Dove onto other brands' (41). The key to that success is the campaign's incorporation of significant elements of consumer co-production from women interacting with the campaign's website; as Banet-Weiser points out, however, this doesn't displace the basic ambiguity that underpins their participation. The contribution of these women's labour to Dove's campaign enables 'both creative activity and exploitation simultaneously' (44).

Such an observation engages with what is now quite a history of debates within the field about the contradictory politics of participatory media of all kinds – from reality TV (Andrejevic, 2004) to micro-celebrity websites (Marwick and boyd, 2011). That history, though, has some twists and turns in it. While the early adopters may have engaged with the highest ideals in mind – the potential for online creativity, the construction of community, and so on – over time they have become more aware of, and progressively more pragmatic about, the corporatisation of these platforms and the monetisation of their participation. It is claimed that users have ultimately resigned themselves to a situation where they implicitly agree to contribute their labour – or more recently, their data – as the price of connectedness (van Dijck, 2013: 158). It is not then a simple opposition between the empowering and expressive potential of these media (Bruns, 2008), and the commercial exploitation of those contributing their labour (Terranova, 2000); both of these remain genuine (and, as Banet-Weiser says, 'simultaneous') capacities of participatory media. The contradiction is in fact constitutive, and it is a consequence of how connective media have evolved in association with egalitarian or communitarian ideals *as well as* with a culture of commercial entrepreneurism.

Among the enabling conditions for this novel ideological partnership is what van Dijck describes as 'the seamless amalgamation of online platforms and mass media into one and the same connective economy' (van Dijck, 2013: 130), echoing Couldry's comment, quoted in the Introduction, that it is the 'interface between interpersonal media and the old mass media that is the most radical change under way' at present. There are all kinds of consequences for the standard categories from within the mass media paradigm that flow from the development of this interface. What we mean when we talk of a 'public', an 'audience', a 'network', or even 'a community',[1] for example, is now far less agreed than was previously the case. Marwick distinguishes the 'broadcast audience' from a 'networked audience' (the networked audience is connected to each other), while insisting that we should not refer to the viewers of 'a piece of digital content' as a public; it is, rather, an audience (Marwick, 2013; 212).[2] While Couldry describes micro-celebrities' engagement in 'sustaining a public presence', he also acknowledges Daniel Miller's problematisation of the use of 'public' in this context, with Miller preferring to describe the 'public' dimension of Facebook as 'an aggregate of private spheres' (Couldry, 2012: 50.) Nancy Baym explores some of the contradictions in linking the networked media to the formation of online 'communities', that comes from 'a shift away from tightly bounded communities towards increasing *networked individualism* in which each person sits at the centre of his or her own personal community' (Baym, 2010: 91). As she points out, this kind of formation might seem 'empowering in terms of sharing and interactivity', but it falls well short of constituting what we might otherwise think of as a community because 'it challenges many of the qualities that can make these groups cohere into something more than the sum of their parts': the network has no sense of place, its behavioural norms are difficult to maintain, the identity of the group is elusive, and so on (ibid.).

Another example of the complications introduced by this expanded and multi-platformed media system is the difficulty that arises when we now try to define once unproblematic terms such as 'television'. With content produced for television now available via the online catch-up services of their originating channel, via downloads or streaming from video aggregator sites, and via numerous mobile devices, there is the question of whether or not television describes a particular content or, more narrowly, a specific platform for distribution and consumption. Michael Newman's history of video argues that 'video' has become the generic label for the content we might once have called television. Newman lists the various locations where video has become the default term for audio-visual screen content: for example, on the iPod and the iPad, on desktop computer menus, as a search term for video-on-demand in cable and satellite programme guides, and in naming the products distributed by Netflix, Hulu and so on. The ubiquity of the term leads him to conclude that 'digital video is the format for movies, television shows, web videos and whatever audio-visual texts fail to match these categories. It is, more and more, the [term for the] moving image' (Newman, 2014: 77).

What drives Newman's history of video into the present is an underlying story about the decline of the mass media. However, as I will go on to argue a little later in this chapter, it is important not to confuse the decline of the mass media paradigm with the decline in the media's centrality or in its power:

> [I]n the multiple-outlet digital media era, 'centrality' becomes an even more important claim for media institutions to make, as they seek to justify the wider 'value' they provide. The ability to speak for, and link audiences to, the 'mediated centre' becomes all the more important, even as its reference points in social and political reality become more tenuous. (Couldry, 2012: 23)

This, in a context where there is a dual process going on: one which, on the one hand, acknowledges the 'actual evaluative and organisational plurality of everyday life' but which still, on the other hand, registers 'the universalising force of media discourse in everyday life' (65).

All of which suggests the need for closer, more instantiated scrutiny of what functions the media now actually serves in all its spheres of operation. While there certainly are examples of such scrutiny, of course, and I will draw upon them throughout this book, it is nonetheless the case that, as I argued in the Introduction, a disproportionate number of these have used new media as their primary reference point. While many have focused solely on the affordances of new media, rather than on broader issues, there are certainly some who have focused their attention on the issue of new media's cultural function; a central approach for many of these has been through the concept of convergence. I have reservations about the usefulness of this approach for understanding the re-invention of the media, and so this is what I want to discuss in the next section of this chapter.

Convergence

In Western, media-intensive, societies such as the UK and the US, the term 'convergence' became quite a buzzword over the early 2000s. As it was commonly applied at the time, it referred to the blurring of the differences between media and telecommunications platforms that came with the arrival of the digital, and the complex of networked interfaces enabled by Web 2.0. Initially, the term circulated most actively among trend-spotters within the media industries and telcos before migrating into the language of those working in media, communications and cultural policy who were charged with modifying the existing regulatory environments to accommodate these new media developments and their capabilities. Policy-makers faced what looked like, from their perspective, a clear break with the era of traditional mass communications: the regulatory structures established to deal with terrestrial national media and communications systems were not going to be able to deal with the coming of the digital world. Those of us in cultural and media studies who were dealing with media policy debates at the time (mostly, this was in the UK and Australia) were continually presented with convergence as a coming 'fact', and asked to provide advice on how to deal with a radically different future for media production, consumption and, thus, for media regulation (Cunningham and Flew, 2002; Turner and Cunningham, 2002).

While convergence might have started out as a relatively instrumentalist concept, adopted as a means of coming to grips with the changing infrastructures for media production, distribution and consumption, once it spread beyond the domain of media and communications policy debate it was integrated into an idealistic popular narrative of 'techno-utopianism' (Newman, 2014: 83) that was marked by its hyperbole. According to one example, convergence was not only the key to describing the economic, technological and cultural changes that marked the new mediascape, it amounted to a change in the human condition (!): '[t]he new human condition, when seen through the lens of those in the forefront of changes in the way work and life are implicated in our increasingly participatory culture, is convergent' (Deuze, 2007: 74). Convergence was endowed with a progressive political provenance – it was democratising, empowering and, according to such projections as Chris Anderson's (2004, 2006) 'long tail' theory, industrially transformative in its implications for the traditional market dominance of mainstream media organisations. In its most parochial iterations, it normatised the conclusions drawn from a limited and at times even anomalous selection of evidence; in others, such as in Meikle and Young's (2012) *Media Convergence*, however, there was a better understanding of the geographic and infrastructural differences in play globally, as well as the need to address the ways in which convergence affected the everyday lives of ordinary consumers, not just those of the fans, the 'techies' and the early adopters.

In my view, however, the expanding range of applications for the term eventually becomes implausible. While otherwise measured in their account, Meikle and Young choose to describe reality TV as a 'convergent media event', for instance, whereas those working on television would describe it, more accurately in my view, as a multi-platform format – a description which acknowledges not only the different platforms available, but also the fact that the individual consumer actively chooses among the range of options provided in terms of the purpose and context of their consumption and how they relate to the specific capacities of each platform. It really only makes sense to describe the shifts in media industry infrastructures as convergent if one privileges the technologies in play; a political economist would be more inclined to describe these industries in terms of increasing concentration or corporate conglomeration. Furthermore, as Andreas Hepp (2013) has noted, 'today's media cultures are not simply cybercultures' (28), and the effective normatisation of the most highly developed digital and networked cultures overstates their relevance to most of the other media users around the globe.

That said, when it finally got around to it, media and cultural studies was enthusiastic about confronting the issue of consumption in the digital era, and about properly interrogating the varying ways in which these media platforms were actually being used by citizens and consumers. Henry Jenkins' (2006) *Convergence Culture* is one of the first, and certainly one of the most influential, attempts to address the challenge of understanding the cultural implications of these new technologies, and opens the way into an examination of the practices of use and consumption that were developing around them. Jenkins is clearly aware of the dangers of 'techno-utopianism', as well as the folly in complacently assuming that 'democracy is an inevitable outcome of technological change' (223). Nonetheless, there is a sense in which his account of convergence culture remains embedded within the phenomenon it describes. *Convergence Culture* seems to speak both about and for a cultural formation that draws its framing discourses from the elite technological entrepreneurs that Marwick (2013) describes, the communitarian tech-fans and early adopters within the US, and the more optimistic end of cultural studies' approaches to the active audience that includes in its prehistory Jenkins' (1992) own *Textual Poachers*. The book has thus proven vulnerable to those who criticise it for the national and geo-cultural specificity of its frame of reference. While some of that criticism is unfair in my view (Meikle and Young describe it as a contribution to 'the literature of fan studies' rather than anything of broader significance [Meikle and Young, 2012: 6]), the book's concentration on fans and tech-savvy users in the US does limit just what general conclusions can legitimately be drawn from that evidence. There is now a body of critical work, including my own (Turner, 2011b), which takes issue with this and with other aspects of Jenkins' approach.[3] Nonetheless, notwithstanding the extent of *Convergence Culture*'s influence on the field, as well as the widespread use of Jenkins' work as the straw man for critical engagement, what is now an extensive critique of the notion of convergence culture is a response to the broader theoretical and cultural formation that has developed around it, rather than only or specifically to Jenkins' contribution.

That critique is substantial. For a start, most of the industry projections proposed by the 'digital optimists' have turned out to be wrong. Elberse's (2014) analysis of the effect of digital downloads on the music industry, for instance, rather than providing evidence of Anderson's 'long tail', reveals a massive degree of market concentration (in 2011, of the 8 million tracks sold in North America, 95 per cent sold fewer than 100 copies). As one newspaper review of Elberse's book put it, 'if, like Chris Anderson, you thought a better world was riding in on the back of broadband, you were, I'm afraid, wrong' (Appleyard, 2014). Furthermore, the idea that there is something uniquely democratising about convergent media is even less convincing when viewed from a longer historical perspective. In terms that precisely foreshadow the claims made for digital media, Michael Newman describes how second-phase home video (that is, video as it developed over the period from the late 1960s through to the early 1990s, including camcorders, home taping, video rentals and so on) was 'often positioned similarly to cable ... as a liberating, culturally uplifting and democratizing medium. It promised to be a kind of Robin Hood of media, redistributing power in communication from corporations and institutions to individuals' (Newman, 2014: 25). If that sounds familiar, even more familiar should be the claim that home video would enable media audiences to 'program their own cultural experiences rather than merely choosing from a small set of culturally degraded options offered through the limited commercial channels' (ibid.).

Projections that suggested user-generated content would deliver a new world of audience empowerment have not withstood close inspection. The scale of participation that actually occurred was always out of proportion to the scale of the claims being made for its significance (Lovink, 2008: xxvii), and the possibility that many of these new 'voices' would actually be heard has turned out to be minimal (Hindman, 2009). Moreover, it was not appropriate to simply read off a politics of empowerment from the mere fact of participation. As Banet-Weiser (2012) points out, the most optimistic accounts 'often rely on a limited, binaristic understanding of participation – say, whether or not one posts a video'. As she explains in her discussion of young girls' use of online personal profiles, the politics of their participation is more ambiguous than that:

> [T]his is especially evident within the public performance of girls' personal lives – the communicative act involved in self-disclosure works as a technique of self-branding, thus objectifying young women precisely through the act of authorizing them as subjects. (82)

Similar points were made in relation to the phenomenon of the 'cam-girls' in the early to mid-2000s, where their ventures into self-disclosure placed the cam-girls in close proximity to porn sites (Senft, 2008; Turner, 2004). On a broader societal level, the exorbitance of the social and political projections associated with convergence culture prompts Mark Andrejevic (2013) to point out, perhaps equally provocatively, that there is actually little evidence that 'the emergence of participatory forms of interactivity has coincided with widespread forms of economic or political empowerment':

> On the contrary, the early decades of convergence culture coincided with the dramatic concentration of economic power in the US, increasing income disparity, and profound challenges to public accountability by the executive branch, security agencies and commercial entities. (60–61)

For my purposes here, the core weakness of the literature on convergence culture, and it is in my view a weakness that seriously limits its usefulness for the broad project of rethinking media theory right now, is that it is more or less blind to the role played by the commercial interests that are implicated in – indeed, that drive – these developments. Where these interests are acknowledged, their association with a 'cool', grassroots, communitarian, connectivity culture has, in effect, 'cleansed them of their association with capital' (Turner 2010). As Lovink (2013) suggests, (and as Robert McChesney [2007] keeps on telling us) the perspective that is missing here is that of political economy. Andrejevic (2013) has tracked the close discursive alignment between the positions taken by many of those engaged with building the academic literature on convergence culture, and by those who seek to profit from marketing these developments – as both sectors embrace the ability for consumers to make their voices heard via interactive technologies. However, while these two parties might well be equally enthusiastic, and for what might seem like the same reasons, their interests are very different. The connectedness that consumers seek out, both to one another and to larger communities, might indeed be delivered at the level of the individual transaction, but, viewed from a more macro perspective, it is clear that their participation has, by and large, been 'coopted' by media corporations (Holt and Sanson, 2014: 7). Rather than the creators of new media technology 'tilting' their developments towards individuals' interests instead of those of the commercial or government spheres, a 'ruthlessly commercial logic' now dominates the 'emergent digital world' (Turow, 2011: 14). This logic is effectively masked by the practices of connectivity in which consumers engage every day, and which seem to tell a different story. However, rather than power being generated through the participation of consumers with shared interests, it is progressively being located in the media corporations' operation of 'search algorithms that assemble conversations and posts about particular brands and topics' (Andrejevic, 2013: 55). Despite its counterculture ethos, and despite its idealistic discourses of participation and empowerment, convergence culture is 'deeply rooted in contemporary capitalism' (Marwick, 2013: 5).

I have a further reservation about the concept of convergence culture, however, which is quite fundamental. I remain unconvinced that what actually occurs between users and these technologies is best described as convergence. When viewed from 'above', and focused entirely on the technologies in play, it does seem as if there are a lot of platforms doing a lot of more or less the same thing – hence, indeed, convergence. Or, rather, when considered from the point of view of the media's production, I agree it is clear that those working in the media industries today require a portfolio of skills that enables them to work across multiple platforms rather than solely within a specific medium: I am thinking here of writing, video production and Web-design as skill-bases that are now required across most if not all media platforms right now. However, when viewed from 'below', and rather focusing on the practices of consumption, things look considerably different. Once we examine how audiences or consumers actually use these technologies, I think we see more *divergence* than convergence. In relation to social media, but also in relation to the changing patterns of television consumption in the post-broadcast environment, the evidence suggests that users make differentiated and individualised choices that are highly responsive to context: these choices have specific cultural, social, economic and geo-political – rather than merely technological or infrastructural – determinants. (Gerson's [2010] *The Breakup 2.0* provides us with an extended demonstration of this, through its examination of young people's choice of media practices when terminating romantic relationships.) As Madaniou and Miller put it in their account of what they describe as 'polymedia' – the aggregation of social media capacities for interpersonal communication – this is 'about a new set of social relations of technology, rather than merely a technological development of increased convergence' (Madaniou and Miller, 2013: 171).

Among the findings of the transnational comparative research I referred to in the Introduction (Turner and Tay, 2009; Pertierra and Turner, 2013) was how persistently and thoroughly media consumption was framed by the specific patterns of everyday life within each of the locations under consideration. The diversity of the structures of media provision and availability across the locations examined – in Asia, Latin America, the US and the UK – was marked. We also noted just how specific and strategically motivated were the actual patterns of choices made in each location. What we found was not the steady convergence of media technologies we might have expected from the convergence culture literature, but rather the stubbornly contingent *hybridisation* of media platforms and the social (importantly, not just the personal) customisation of their cultures of use as they were adapted to the broad socio-cultural frames that made up the context of consumption. In dealing with a process which effectively socialises these technologies (Madaniou and Miller, 2013) in a highly contextualised manner, hybridity seems like a more useful, because more accurately descriptive, concept than convergence. Social media is an illustration of this: social media is marked by its hybridised capacities and deployment – mixing the interpersonal with the one-to-many functions of the mass media, but with the consumer often able to determine the settings for the precise blend of the various capacities they use. At the simplest level, the concept of convergence is almost inevitably focused on the technologies, whereas the concept of hybridity highlights the instantiated practices of use and therefore takes us more directly to questions of the cultural, the social and the political function of the media.

David Morley, some years ago now, was among the first to call for a less 'media-centric' account of the media (Morley, 2007: 200). This objective had two key elements: one was to remind media studies of the need to focus upon how media use was embedded within broader social practices, and the other was to turn away from accounts that were only concerned with a specific media technology. With the decline of the mass media paradigm, it has become even more important for cultural and media studies to seek empirical evidence about how people actually use the media. The shifts in technology have to find their place within the existing structures of people's habits and practices of consumption, and these are in turn located within histories of everyday life that play a fundamental role in determining the function of the media – for 'these' people, with 'these' media options, in 'this' place and at 'this' time.

Consumption studies is one approach which has grown in influence within cultural and media studies more generally, and it does provide us with useful examples of non-media-centric accounts which locate the media firmly within the social. Madaniou and Miller's (2013) work on polymedia is an instance of this. Their research examines media use by migrants and focuses on how their informants select the appropriate media platform as a means of staying in touch with family and friends in their country of origin. Madaniou and Miller find that for typical groups of these individuals there are a range of technologies available: landlines, mobile or cell-phones, computers using VOIPs such as Skype, as well as connectivity platforms such as email, social media and so on. What interests Madaniou and Miller is how purposefully and contingently their subjects make their choices from this 'emerging environment of communicative opportunities'. While the whole repertoire of available choices operates as 'an integrated structure', each choice is made in order to access particular sets of affordances. These are chosen by their users for their perceived suitability, not so much in terms of the 'qualities of each particular medium as a discrete technology', but more in terms of the kind of social relations they enable:

> As a consequence, the primary concern shifts from an emphasis on the constraints imposed by each medium (often cost-related but also shaped by specific qualities) to an emphasis upon the social and emotional consequences of choosing between these different media. We will argue that navigating the environment of polymedia becomes inextricably linked to the ways in which interpersonal relationships are enacted and experienced. As a consequence, polymedia in effect helps to re-socialize the technology, since the responsibility of choice

shifts from technical and economic, to moral, social and emotional concerns.
(Madaniou and Miller, 2013: 170–171)

Importantly, while Madaniou and Miller maintain the distinctions between the capacities of particular media platforms, they connect these distinctions to the practices of the users rather than regarding them as an intrinsic attribute of the platform. When their subjects choose to use email rather than Skype, for instance, to communicate with their parents, that is partly to do with the technical capacities involved – in some cases email was chosen precisely because the sender cannot be seen, for instance – but is more to do with the purpose of the communication for the individual concerned (making personal contact, while exercising higher levels of control over the content and implications of the communication). Unlike the convergence culture theorists, then, Madaniou and Miller do not see the media as a convergent space but, on the other hand, neither do they simply take the 'media-centric' option of analysing each medium as a discrete technology. The emphasis is upon the social, and upon the active choices being made by consumers.

Mediatisation

A significant body of work on the relations between the media, the social and the cultural that has emerged from Europe, and in particular from Scandinavia, over the last five years takes the opposite approach to that outlined in the polymedia project: it could be described as setting out to explain how *the media itself* operates as a socialising force. This theoretical development responds to what has variously been described as 'mediation'(Livingstone, 2009; Couldry, 2013) or 'mediatisation' (Hepp, 2013; Hjarvard, 2013); there are slight differences between the uses of these two terms, but it is the latter term I am going to deal with here. The development of theories of mediatisation is what Stig Hjarvard (2013: 4) describes as a 'long range' project aimed at understanding precisely how the media participates in, perhaps even constructs, the social. It, too, rejects a media-centric orientation. While Andreas Hepp, for example, argues that our culture has been 'transformed into a media culture', the idea of a media culture is not just about what is represented in the media, nor is it about merely mapping the transition from one media form to another – narratives that have us leaving the 'era of the book or of the television and entering the bright new world of the internet' (Hepp, 2013: 2). Rather, it is about understanding how culture is 'moulded' by the media (ibid.). Drawing on Schmidt's work, Hepp argues that 'the traditional distinction made between experiences conveyed through media and those which are not becomes irrelevant, since the cultures of mediatization we live in today', he suggests, are thoroughly, inherently, 'saturated with media communication' (Hepp, 2013: 128).

Central to this diagnosis (and its implications return us once more to our consideration of the decline of the mass media paradigm) is an account of the changing institutional roles performed by the contemporary media in the democratic nation-states in the West. Hjarvard argues that a significant proportion of the influence that the media exert arises out of the double-sided development in which they have become an *integral* part of other institutions' operations, while also achieving a degree of *self-determination and authority* that forces other institutions, to greater and lesser degrees to submit to their logic. (Hjarvard, 2013: 3)

The media are institutionally contained and embedded, then, while also behaving as independent social actors with sufficient power to influence the actions of others. Organised party politics is probably the most obvious example of this latter process. The notion that the media now have their own 'logic' has attracted some debate, however. Couldry, for instance, argues that it is 'difficult to see a single logic which would explain the range of general effects to which mediatisation theorists claim to point' (Couldry, 2012: 136). Like Couldry, I am not convinced there is such a single identifiable entity, either, although I recognise that the more general structural shifts Hjarvard describes do resonate with my earlier argument (Turner, 2010) that the media now no longer 'mediate', but have their own interests and uses for power.

Once we go past relatively straightforward evidence of the media's direct participation in social change, such as the way in which the use of mobile phones has changed certain aspects of social relations (Hepp, 2013), the task of developing a research approach through which we might examine mediatisation in practice – in particular the work of 'moulding' culture – remains a work in progress. Mediatisation theory is at an 'early stage' and it is not even clear as yet if it should 'necessarily' be 'aiming at the development of a definitive concept' (Hjarvard, 2013: 4). It has an ambitious theoretical agenda, though, as it seeks ways to 'study the manner in which the moulding develops, the kinds of changes in communication that occur and hence, the way in which [social] reality is constructed' (Hepp, 2013: 68). Cultural and media studies has been here before, of course, in the days of ideology critique, when we carefully interrogated the politics of representation for the way in which it interpellated us into particular constructions of the real. Such work, however, was not specifically about the role of the media; rather, media texts were used as convenient and productive (rather than privileged or determining) locations for the analysis of larger cultural and meaning-making processes – ultimately, for the operation of language, itself. For its part, mediatisation theory focuses on the sociocultural function of the media as its primary object of analysis. It gains its importance from the dramatic changes we have been discussing in the structure and function of the media in everyday life, and because it sets out to understand how the contemporary media is embedded in social practice and in the construction of social identities (Hjarvard, 2013: 11).

Interestingly, much of what mediatisation theory deals with is actually the operation of the mass media, but similar accounts of the changing social role of media come from those who have focused on the culture of connectivity. For van Dijck, media technologies actually 'mature' as part of everyday social practices – just as Madaniou and Miller suggest, they become 'socialised'. Therefore, van Dijck says, 'as a medium coevolves with its quotidian users' tactics, it contributes to shaping people's everyday life, while at the same time this mediated sociality becomes part of society's institutional fabric' (van Dijck, 2013: 5–6). For Nick Couldry, adapting Bourdieu's field theory to the task of understanding these relations, media generates a kind of 'meta-capital' across cultural fields that 'extends beyond media's direct influence over capital to include a more indirect influence that works through the media's legitimation of influential *representations of*, and *categories for*, understanding the social world' (Couldry, 2012: 141). Now, while there are notes struck in such comments that may be familiar from earlier cultural studies accounts of the relation between the media, representation and culture, there is another thread which runs through them – and it is one which also links them to the mediatisation arguments. That is, the strong sense that we have entered unfamiliar territory as we try to explain the contemporary function of a media landscape through using a map of contingent social relations that has dramatically expanded, that has fractured the mass media model which anchored earlier accounts, and which is throwing up instances of development, change and disruption more quickly than we can assimilate them. While we can discern a consensus about the emergence of new kinds of institutionalised power, we can also sense the hesitation that haunts many of these contemporary explanations of what this power is, and how it works. If the media has been re-invented: if it is no longer primarily a mediating force, and if it now has its own interests and uses for power; if its uses have mutated and hybridised as new platforms emerge, and if it is now even more comprehensively (while more diversely) implicated in the structures of the everyday, the normal and the routine; then clearly it is worth looking into what this means for the production of culture and the formation of the social. Media and cultural studies urgently need to reconsider our understandings of the constitution and operation of media power.

Commercialisation, the public good and media power

One important step (and it is only one among a number of possibilities) towards such a reconsideration, and a move that pushes back against the grain of the more optimistic accounts, would be to more fully acknowledge the socio-political implications of the increased commercialisation of the media. An earlier default understanding of the media – this, even when many of them were in fact commercially operated – regarded them as 'cultural institutions, in the sense of institutions that, in the public interest, represent the entire society to a general public' (Hjarvard, 2013: 23). As more media systems have been privatised and as media markets have become more globalised and more structured around commercial competition, this is no longer so apposite. Instead, the typical media organisation in the West today is an enterprise with a strong market orientation focused sharply on 'servicing' its own audiences and users who are now more strategically and individually targeted. The notion of the public good which might once have operated as a buffer against commercial imperatives, thus moderating the influence of the interests of the media organisation itself, is in decline; what now counts as professional practice within journalism, for instance – once the epitome of how the media served the public interest – is more to do with the demands of the industry than with serving the public good (Hjarvard, 2013: 26). Joseph Turow's account of the new world of advertising, in which new marketing and media-buying strategies are acquiring the 'capacity to determine not only what media firms do but how we see ourselves and others' (Turow, 2011: 8), is a further example where the commercial interests of these organisations are pursued in ways that will generate significant social consequences, as the unintended and unexamined by-products of the methods chosen to generate a profit.

What Turow (2011) is talking about in *The Daily You* is largely the adoption of sophisticated tracking and targeting strategies, which focus on individuals as the object of marketing. Such strategies are presented to consumers as a service, of course, as a means of ensuring we are well informed about the products and services we are most likely to want to buy. The potentials for individualisation, customisation and personalisation are offered as benefits to the consumer, but less is said about the benefits flowing to the media corporation as a result of their harnessing of consumer participation. There is a familiar process now which shapes how digital media, particularly connective media, develop their markets. Typically, they are initially offered to consumers as an open 'utility', often at no charge, but they soon mutate into operating as a 'customized service – so, no longer a *conduit* for social activity, but rather the provision of *applied services*' that usually then attract a fee (van Dijck, 2013: 6). While 'connectedness' may initially serve as the core attractor for the consumer, data generation has become the primary commercial objective, rather than the by-product, for the provider (12). After the socialisation of these technological affordances, then, comes their monetisation; and this is closely followed by a refocusing of their capacities upon the commercial objectives of the organisation rather than upon the personal interests of the users. The histories of YouTube or of Facebook, for instance, provide clear examples of this. So, typically, and against all the early expectations, the power that was initially offered to the individual as the benefit of connectedness ends up, in effect, being transferred back (ironically, directly by that individual's participation) to the corporations and institutions who run the media.

The commercial capture of social media has been comprehensive; at the same time, it has been either disavowed or overlooked in much of the associated literature – thus perpetuating the illusion that these platforms are primarily focused upon delivering a grassroots, communitarian connectivity. While, as I say, this is only one of the issues requiring more attention, and we will deal with a number of others in this book, it is nonetheless a crucial one. Media and cultural studies' assessment of the power relations involved in the contemporary media needs to more thoroughly acknowledge and respond to the situation van Dijck describes:

> A quick look at today's palette of the 100 biggest social media platforms reveals that the overwhelming majority (almost 98 per cent) are run by corporations who think of the Internet as a market-place first and as a public forum second – Wikipedia being the most notable exception. And yet the rhetoric of

a new public sphere was (and still is to some extent) gratefully appropriated by businesses to salvage the virtues of the corporate sphere (van Dijck, 2013: 18).

To make this argument properly would require the kind of research Geert Lovink (2013) is calling for, an investigation into the political economy of social media monopolies. One could confidently predict, however, that any political economy of these organisations would find that it strongly resembled the broader political economy of a transnationally concentrated mainstream media. It would not be surprising to find that, in this respect, the power of mainstream media has remained more or less unaffected by the media's re-invention (Freedman, 2006).

Indeed, viewed from another perspective, one could actually argue that in some ways the media's power has been extended. The commercialisation of the media I have described simplifies the media's project: it can be ideologically and politically flexible in ways that may not have been possible before. Zala Volcic's (2009, 2013) examination of what she describes as 'commercial nationalism' provides us with examples of the media working with the tools available to generate a commercial outcome and, along the way, as a by-product, a version of national identity. Volcic presents case studies of how commercial television in some of the nation-states emerging from the former Yugoslavia has cynically appropriated regional discourses of ethno-nationalism as a means of creating an audience for its reality TV formats. This both exploits and feeds into a concurrent state-supported process of nation-branding as well as into the long-running histories of ethno-racial antagonisms in the region. However, what is different in this situation to those which might have obtained earlier, is the degree to which something as culturally significant as the media's participation in the construction of a national identity is motivated by commercial, rather than political or cultural, considerations. For these commercial TV proprietors, the engagement with defining discourses of national identity is a means, not an end. Such a deployment of media power is more politically agile because it is also more politically agnostic due to the single-mindedness of its focus on commercial benefit.

What Volcic's work highlights is the persistence of a form of power that seemed initially to have declined with the rise of social media, user-generated content and the like: this is what Bourdieu (1991: 166) called 'symbolic power' – the power to construct social reality – or what John Thompson has described as 'the capacity to intervene in the course of events, to influence the actions of others, and indeed to create events, by means of the production and transmission of symbolic forms' (Thompson, 1995: 17), Nick Couldry, usefully, provides us with an outline of his view of the manner in which symbolic power constructs the social. While all forms of power, he argues, work in a 'dispersed' way, 'symbolic power impacts upon wider society more pervasively than other forms of power (such as economic power) because the concentration of society's symbolic resources affects not just what we do but our ability to *describe* whatever "goes on"' (Couldry, 2012: 87). It is a similar process to that described by those developing the concept of mediatisation: while the media has the discursive capacity to define how reality is constructed, this is not just at the level of specific patterns of representation – it is broader, more banal and more habit- and practice-based than that. Couldry, among others, argues that the concentration of symbolic power within the media is a serious political issue because its uneven distribution distorts the representation of social facts, and the construction of social space. As a result, the concentration of symbolic power within the media is 'intrinsically divisive' (Couldry, 2012: 89), separating those with access to this power from those without. In fact, it is precisely this division we had once hoped that connective media, the rise of citizen journalism and all the supposedly democratising developments of the last decade or two would address and remedy.

However, Mirca Madaniou, writing about the implications of the tabloid newspaper phone-hacking scandal in the UK, argues that digital media, with their enhanced capacities for sharing, copying and so on, may even have pushed aspirations of this kind further back as it has also expanded the capacity for the media to inflict 'new forms of harm'. In the digital era, offensive or intrusive online news content 'is no longer ephemeral', as it might have been in the heyday of the newspaper, but permanently retrievable, potentially for ever. The consequent increase in the potential scale of the audience attending to the message amplifies the harmful effects for the exposed individual (Madaniou, 2013: 193) While it might be tempting to see the 'talking back' capacities of social media as offering some remedy to this, Madaniou throws cold water on that possibility, specifically in terms of the uneven distribution of symbolic power involved; social media may, she says, 'provide a platform for wronged subjects to speak back and address their audiences in a more direct way, but social media without social and symbolic capital are not likely to provide a platform for voice' (ibid.).

A key concern for me at the present conjuncture is what I regard as the relative lack of attention given by current cultural and media studies to interrogating the manner in which the interests of media institutions and organisations have shaped the re-invention of the media over the last two decades. We need to know more about what constitutes media power in the current era, how that power is used, and in whose interests. There are plenty of others, of course, who share similar objectives in their own work on particular aspects of the contemporary media, and part of the syncretic project of this book is to bring some of those arguments together, to remove some of the disaggregation of analysis that has come with the fragmentation of focus in media studies that has resulted from the recurring need to investigate emerging media platforms.

I want to conclude this chapter by turning to Joseph Turow's account of changes to the advertising industry where, towards the end of his book, he addresses what must remain among the most significant political questions we, as media, communications and cultural studies scholars, should be asking – What does a society need from its media?

> I would suggest that a good society should have a balance between what might be called society-making media and segment-making media. Segment-making

media are media that encourage small sections of society to talk to themselves, while society-making media are those that have the potential to get all those segments to talk to each other. A hallmark of the twentieth century was the growth of both types in the United States. A huge number of ad-supported vehicles – mostly magazines and newspapers – served as a way to reinforce, even create, identities for an impressive array of segments that advertisers cared about, from immigrant Czechs to luxury-car owners, to Knights of Columbus, and far more. At the same time, some ad-sponsored newspapers, radio networks, and – especially – television networks were able to reach across those groups. Through entertainment, news and information, society-making media depicted concerns and connections that people ought to share in a larger national community. (Turow, 2011: 193)

This is not a currently fashionable set of principles; after all, these days we keep on being told that the media now works for *us*. But, it is a salutary reminder of what should be core concerns for cultural and media studies. Turow acknowledges both the necessity of serving the media's commercial interests while also serving something like the public good; he recognises the scale of the media's symbolic power while also insisting on an ethical and political interrogation of how that power is used. It would be good to see more of that kind of orientation in contemporary analysis of the media.

The re-invention of the media has dramatically reconfigured what 'counts' as media, and in doing so has precipitated the declining centrality of the mass media paradigm. The power of the media has been reconfigured as well. Turow's two models – of a segment-making media and a society-making media – are both now subservient to a media system that is, more than ever before, a 'profit-making' media. What has blurred our view of this gradual consolidation of media power across platforms as they emerge and seek the means of monetisation, is the success with which media proprietors and corporations have represented their investment in new media platforms – in connective media most significantly, but also in multi-channel television, digital radio, reality TV and the rise of the ordinary celebrity – as an opening up of the media to the audience, and of designing the affordances of media platforms in accordance with the interests of their audiences. The reality is much more politically compromised than that, as the dialectic between exploitation and empowerment has become a fundamentally constitutive feature of the contemporary media's relation with ordinary people. The media have at least retained, if not even extended, their symbolic power because their re-invention has taken place in such close association with the social that it now carries major consequences for the ways in which our social life, and our perspectives on our social life, are constructed. We can already see mediatised shifts in consumers' attitudes to personal privacy, to the presentation and performance of the self, and in changes to the practices through which we manage interpersonal communication (and we will discuss each of these in later chapters). The re-invention of the media affects far more than merely our choices in entertainment or communication; it carries with it the potential for the re-invention of what, and how, we think about our everyday lives as well.

Notes

1 In *Locating Television* (Pertierra and Turner, 2013), Anna Pertierra and I have a chapter which deals with the varying notions of community, in particular as taken up within accounts of new media.
2 Marwick (2013: 212) explains that the term 'audience' 'can refer to the imagined audience, the actual audience, or the potential audience for one's content'. But while 'potential audience' resembles the vernacular sense of 'public', she uses 'audience' to mean 'the actual audience, the people interested in a piece of information who actually view it'.
3 There has been a special issue of *Cultural Studies* (2011, 25: 4–5) which was devoted to 'reconsidering convergence/culture' as a broad theoretical formation, although some of the essays it contains do focus in particular on Jenkins' book.

2

ENTERTAINMENT, INFORMATION AND THE 'CULTURE OF SEARCH'

Among the standard rubrics historically used to describe the desired function of the traditional mass media was the Reithian triplet – the media were there to inform, educate and entertain. This desire is now looking more and more anachronistic as the media goes about re-inventing itself. Today, as the traditional mass media have sought ways to respond to the challenges to their longstanding dominance, as the media's thoroughgoing privatisation has reconfigured its relation to the interests of the state, and as digital media create markets where none had previously existed, there are large sections of the media which are not interested in education at all, and other sections which have chosen to distance themselves from the responsibility for informing the public. Perhaps some might argue that, even in the mass media era, this has always been the case – and they would have a point. However, what I think *has* changed is that this latter tendency seems to be most marked in precisely the domain where education and information were once regarded as fundamental, and where the media's social responsibilities were held to be most central: the production of news and current affairs. As consumer access to news and information online has dramatically expanded, the traditional news media have sought to retain their audiences by committing more resources to categories of content other than those which might have previously been regarded as news. As we shall see in more detail in Chapter 6, what constitutes news has significantly changed as the news media, and indeed the media in general, have engaged in a process of redefining themselves as platforms for entertainment. Among the consequences of the media's progressive commercialisation, in a context of proliferating platforms for producers and multiplying choices for consumers, is the compelling necessity for all sectors of the media to focus their attention on finding the most effective means of competing for audiences – and this has inevitably resulted in the rise of entertainment and its ascendancy over information as the most marketable regime of content.

In *Ordinary People and the Media* (Turner, 2010), I argued that popular catch-phrases such as 'the information age' or the 'network society' (Castells, 2009) need to be at least complicated by an equivalent acknowledgment of the significance of the rise of entertainment; I suggested that a strong case can be made for labelling the contemporary period 'the entertainment age'. The evidence I might cite extends well beyond the field of news and current affairs; for instance, there is a Deloitte report on the changing function of the home computer, once seen as 'an information, education and organizational tool', which finds that its primary use 'is now for entertainment' (Deloitte, 2009; Turner, 2010: 159). Such an orientation is also inscribed into the shrinking range of affordances available via most versions of the tablet, which shifts it away from the full range of production and consumption we would identify with the desktop or laptop computer (no word processing or spreadsheet programs, for instance) in order to concentrate the tablet's capacities on the consumption of information and entertainment – typically email, search, social media, music, photos and video. Similarly, the design and use of the smart phone is being progressively oriented towards the consumption of entertainment.[1]

I am far from the only one to have made this point in relation to the changing orientation of the news media. In *Media and Democracy* (Curran, 2011), a book I will draw on significantly for the first part of this chapter, James Curran claims that 'in most parts of the world, the news media are becoming more market-oriented and entertainment-centred' (47). Some years earlier, Peter Dahlgren had already noticed this shift in the make-up of the public sphere, suggesting that 'the media, with television in the vanguard' were drifting 'ever further in the direction of entertainment and consumption' (Dahlgren, 2009: 126). Nick Couldry, even more conclusively, claims that the 'shift to entertainment in global media agendas may be the biggest change under way in everyday media use' (Couldry, 2012: 19–20). He points out that there are many good industrial and political reasons for this: 'the dominance of entertainment (a less costly investment than investigative journalism) suits the bottom-line economics of weak media institutions' and, more importantly, entertainment programming has proven highly flexible discursively and is thus readily made compatible with many 'political contexts and outcomes: post-socialist competitive nationalism in the former Yugoslavia; the social/market hybrid politics of China; the fragile democratic politics of post-dictatorship Philippines' (Couldry, 2012: 25).

I think it would be fair to say that there is a relatively widespread acceptance of the position to which I alluded at the beginning of this chapter: that this situation has come about as a consequence of the expansion of the commercial multi-channel market in television, the enthusiasm in some jurisdictions for marketising deregulation, the contraction in the presence and influence of public broadcasting, and the rapid emergence of competing media technologies, platforms and consumer devices. Some also point to the related social and economic shifts that have affected more than the shape of contemporary media. Dahlgren notes that 'as the commercial imperatives of the media have hardened over the past few decades', and as the 'balance between public responsibility and private profit has been steadily tipping in favour of the latter', 'normative goals' for media performance such as those which might have regulated the practices of traditional fourth estate journalism, for instance, have given way to 'economic calculation' (Dahlgren, 2009: 36–37). Natalie Fenton points to the principles underpinning such a development. Even though there has been so much talk about 'pluralisation, and enhanced democracy' in recent years, she says, the dominant forces in the wider world, within which the media must compete, are 'extreme corporatisation, financialisation and privatisation' (Fenton, 2013a: 142).

This chapter asks a number of questions about this situation. First, it considers what might be the cultural and political consequences of such a shift. Specifically, it asks what has happened to the conception of the public good that originally motivated the invocation of education and information as among the primary social responsibilities of the mass media. Second, how are we to reconcile the contradictory implications of the decline of information as a primary component of the content of the news media, when placed against the massive expansion in the access to information provided by the internet; does the latter, for instance, effectively compensate for the former? Does what Hillis, Petit and Jarrett (2013) describe as 'the culture of search' merely provide a location for the discovery of information, or is it rather the place where we see the active, and perhaps even the productive, hybridisation of the Reithian principles invoked above? There is also the question raised by Hillis et al.'s claim that search now constitutes 'a way of life'; at the moment it appears that this 'way of life' may itself be threatened by the churn in industrial innovations generated by commercial competition and the need for better management, targeting and direction of consumer choice – that is, by a culture of apps, which may well wind back some of the perceived benefits of the discovery-oriented search engine. Third, we need to consider the fact that the increase in the accessibility of information online is not without its own constitutive social and political contradictions. The citizen/consumer in many locations now enjoys an unprecedented degree of access to an unlimited supply of information via formats that appear to enable a high degree of customisation to the consumer's needs and interests. While there is good reason to see this new capacity as, in certain respects, a benefit for these consumers, it has also been recognised that such a benefit comes at the cost of, among other things, providing commercial organisations with access to private information that is then commodified and sold. Drawing on the work of Mark Andrejevic and of Joseph Turow, in particular, the chapter finally considers current debates about just how 'empowering' this new world of information is turning out to be, and for whom.

Before moving into this series of questions, however, I need to signal my awareness of the dangers of assuming a simple binary division between information and entertainment – a division that is usually employed as a means of privileging the importance of information (which effectively means the coverage of 'hard news' such as politics) and of dismissing entertainment as trivial. Such a division implies a history in which media platforms could once have been exclusively identified with one or other of these alternatives. The press in the 18th and early 19th centuries may well have 'consisted primarily of highly politicised newspapers and journals' (Curran, 2011: 63), but as the mass market for news developed over the 19th and 20th centuries, such an exclusive focus on politics became less common. Entertainment was central, for instance, to the popular appeal of the muck-raking newspapers in the US at the turn of the 20th century but, as any student of US politics over this period will know, this does not at all mean that these newspapers had little to do with politics. In the contemporary context, Curran argues, specifically in relation to the role of the media in democratic states, even though 'the great bulk of content produced by contemporary media systems' has 'nothing to do with public affairs' or 'conventional understandings of politics' (Curran, 2011: 63), it would be a mistake to assume that entertainment programming plays no part in educating and informing its audience:

> In brief, entertainment connects to the democratic life of society in four ways. It provides a space for exploring and debating social values, which occupy a central place in contemporary politics. It offers a means of defining and refashioning social identity, something that is inextricably linked to a sense of self-interest. It affords alternative frameworks of understanding, which inform public debate. And it provides a way of assessing, strengthening, weakening and revising public norms that are an integral part of the way we govern ourselves. To continue to view entertainment as something removed from politics, and unrelated to the democratic role of the media, is no longer sustainable. (Curran, 2011: 75)

While it has long been customary for media studies to examine how entertainment programming can work to reinforce dominant or elite values and norms, it is also the case, as Couldry argues, that in some cases, 'entertainment may be the most effective way for voices and questions that challenge traditional and elite discourses to break through' (Couldry, 2012: 25). The history of US television is full of examples of this – M*A*S*H* is probably the most obvious instance – and Amanda Lotz's recent *Cable Guys* discusses how contemporary US cable television drama, in particular, has deliberately 'sought characters and narratives that would generate cultural discussion' as a commercial strategy (Lotz, 2014b: 29). Most significantly, Marwan Kraidy's (2010) research on the political function of reality television in the Arab states has provided an extremely powerful analysis of this capacity.

Nonetheless, there is value, as I hope this discussion will demonstrate, in making use of the distinction between entertainment and information in order to describe particular aspects of the shifts involved in the media's re-invention. After all, this is a distinction that still constitutes a fundamental means of structuring the media's production industries and thus their allocation of resources; in most industry configurations, news and entertainment remain organisationally distinct from one another (Havens, Lotz and Tinic, 2009: 250). That said, there is a particular need to be alert to the nuances required, to the assumptions implied, and to the limits to the generalisations that can be made about the media overall, while contextualising this part of my argument. Initially, then, I should emphasise that what I want to argue in the next section relates specifically to the news media, rather than necessarily to the media in general. More importantly, though, I should also emphasise that my interest in the rise of entertainment is not about delivering a critique of a decline in the quality of media content; rather, it is to make use of this shift as a means of engaging a little further with the issue of the media's commercialisation and the effect that this is likely to have upon certain aspects of the media's social function.

News, entertainment and the public good

Let's start with the proposition that the news media (in the West, certainly, but not only there) are more than ever before competing by way of the entertainment, rather than the information, they provide. There are a number of consequences to this development, and I will be looking at one of them – the so-called 'crisis in journalism' – in more detail in Chapter 5. I want to focus here, however, on what Dahlgren described as the 'displacement of the public good with private profit'; the fact that the media are now overwhelmingly focused on their own commercial interests and that these now, I would suggest more categorically and unapologetically than before, take precedence over those of the public or, indeed, of a broad notion of politics.

There is, of course, the danger of signing up to an elegiac 'golden age' narrative here, endorsing a mythology of a glittering past in which the news media heroically served the public interest before addressing the need to make a profit. Fortunately, James Curran has performed the useful task of examining relevant aspects of the history of the US press since the Second World War in order to assess the evidence that there may indeed have been a time when the US news media made its public responsibilities explicit and took them seriously; when there was a strong commitment to ethical journalistic practice; and when there was principled resistance to commercial influence. He argues that there was, indeed, such a moment, and that on this basis the US could legitimately claim to be 'the principal originator and exporter of a great media experiment':

> Its starting point is that the media should be organised as a free-market system on the grounds that any form of public ownership or legal regulation (beyond the barest minimum) endangers media freedom. However, this approach differs from neo-liberalism in that it also argues that the free market can have debilitating effects on the media. Its solution to this double bind – the need to have a free market and to negate its adverse effects without involving the state – is to develop a tradition of professionalism among journalists. In this way, the media can remain free, yet serve the people. (Curran, 2011: 9)

Curran's account of what constitutes a media reform movement that goes back into the nineteenth century, and his analysis of key moments in the successful prosecution of what he describes as 'responsible media capitalism' (14), is based on

Entertainment, information, search culture   43

empirical evidence that this 'golden age' of American journalism – perhaps running from the late 1940s into the 1970s, with the occasional resurgence later on – is not just a myth. It didn't last, however, and by the 1980s, even while 'American journalists basked in the admiration of a growing number of peers around the world', American journalism was heading into decline. The reason, Curran suggests, is 'because the foundation of the American experiment – its partially successful attempt to separate business from journalism – was undermined by increased commercialisation' (21).

This, as we have seen, went hand in hand with greater competition. As Curran acknowledges, when there was only the mass media to divide up the commercial spoils, and when it was organised as an oligopoly, the influence of commercial imperatives was much more muted. As he puts it: 'it was much easier to be high-minded when competition was limited and profitability was assured by a rising volume of advertising' (Curran, 2011: 10). That context, of course, is gone; consequently, there is nothing high-minded about how the current trendsetter among US television networks now delivers their news. Curran describes the role played by Fox News, and the influence of Rupert Murdoch, as leading to a situation where 'partisan journalism' has come to 'occupy a substantial niche in both American television and radio journalism': the content and viewpoints taken by Fox News are orientated so that they echo 'the political prejudices of its principal owner'. 'The rise of this new style of journalism', Curran continues, 'marked the compromising entanglement of American journalism with vested economic power' (23).

Fox News is frequently cited as an example of what happens when journalism renounces its commitment to the ethical responsibilities of the fourth estate, and when opinion takes over from newsgathering as the key strategy for attracting audiences. Fox is also commonly cited as an example of the commercial exploitation, if not the abuse, of media power. The other key reference point for such behaviour is, of course, the British tabloid newspapers or 'redtops' where, as Curran says, 'there is little counterweight to commercial pressure' since these papers are 'dominated by an entertainment oriented rather than professional staff culture' (16). In his recent book describing the phone-hacking scandal in the UK, based on his own investigative reporting for *The Guardian* which pursued this story, Nick Davies paints a chilling picture of the workplace culture in the British tabloids over this period, delivering an angry denunciation of what his profession has become:

> Everything is for sale. Nobody is exempt. What begins to emerge is the internal machinery of a commercial enterprise which has never previously existed, an industry which treats human life itself – the soft tissue of the most private, sensitive moments – as a vast quarry full of raw material to be scooped up and sifted and exploited for entertainment. Back in the 1980s, the *News of the World* had specialised in digging into the privacy of criminals. In the 1990s, enriched by the excavation of Princes Diana's volatile life, they had widened their work to mine the activities of any celebrity, any public figure. Now, they had gone even further. The whole of human life – of anybody, anywhere who

had news value – had become one mass of crude bulk for Andy Coulson's newsroom to extract and refine in a ruthless search for the most intimate, embarrassing, often painful details which could then be converted into precious nuggets for sale in a massive marketplace. (Davies, 2014: 33)

Why should we care about this? One answer lies in the end-product of this professional culture in the UK: a predatory and irresponsible newspaper sector dominated by a single proprietor and, according to Davies' account, exercising political power with a ruthlessness that made both the UK government and the police reluctant to launch prosecutions even when they were aware of the systematic encouragement of criminal practices within the News International newsrooms. At one level, the behaviour produced by competition between the British tabloids was simply that – criminal – and so it is not a matter that requires subtle critique in order for us to find it wanting. It is also an extreme case, and cannot be taken as typical of what most of the news media, in most places, normally does. It does, however, throw into sharp relief the distance we have travelled away from the conventions and protocols which structured the traditional practices of newsgathering.

It is important for media and cultural studies to pay attention, more than it has done in recent times in my view, to the broader issue of how such attitudes to newsgathering affect what is supplied to the public as news, and what the social and political effects can turn out to be:

> British tabloids have responded to their deteriorating economic situation by searching with increasing urgency for news that grabs readers' attention. One time-honoured way of achieving this is to find stories that make readers angry ... This strategy led to a spate of anti-immigrant stories during the 2000s, when anti-immigrant attitudes became more widespread. However, tabloid demand for these stories outstripped supply, leading not just to distortion but outright invention. (Curran, 2011: 16)

The social consequences in this particular instance amount to something like a moral panic about immigrants and asylum seekers that had direct effects upon the lives of innocent and vulnerable people, and exerted an influence on politicians' stances on related issues. These are the political effects of the 'information' published in a media outlet that employs the discourses of news, and still bears some of the cultural authority of news, but which is actually publishing a socially irresponsible form of entertainment with little respect for the ethical protocols of news. In this example, the manner in which the news services have processed their information to turn it into entertainment in order to attract an audience has worked against the public good. While extreme examples in themselves, nonetheless these activities were undertaken in the service of what has become a standard commercial objective for the news media in general.

It is easy, of course, to pick off such obvious targets as Fox News or *The News of the World*. For my purposes here, it is not enough to show that such abuses occur;

rather, I want to establish that there has been sufficient systemic change to predispose the re-invented media, in general, towards such self-interested behaviour, and away from the promotion of the public good. I realise that not everyone would accept that this is the case. In their influential *Comparing Media Systems*, Hallin and Mancini (2004) provide an even-handed summary of the arguments around the proposition that commercialisation might have a negative effect on the services provided by the news media. They appear to see some benefit in the degree to which the media have used their commercialisation to increase their independence from the political system; however, my own view of the effects of commercialisation does not necessarily regard this as a benefit. As Hallin and Mancini themselves acknowledge, the 'social function of journalism' is changed by an orientation towards 'the world of commerce': within such an orientation, 'journalism's main objective is no longer to disseminate ideas and create social consensus around them, but to produce entertainment and information that can be sold to individual consumers' (Hallin and Mancini, 2004: 277). In response, Curran argues that Hallin and Mancini's 'agnosticism about the effect of commercialisation on the provision of public affairs information is misplaced' (46) and supports his position by reporting on a research project he conducted which tested the proposition that more market-oriented systems foster less 'serious' kinds of journalism that limit citizens' knowledge of public affairs. The research involved surveying public awareness of various events, issues and individuals in the news in the US, the UK, Denmark and Finland. Among the results that Curran notes from this research (and I am not going into Curran's evidence for this, but it is outlined at length in his book) was the 'relatively high level of public ignorance in America about the wider world and about public life in general'. This, given the fact that 'a growing number of countries are converging towards the entertainment-centred model of American television', 'seems set to foster', he goes on to suggest, 'an impoverished public life characterised by declining exposure to serious journalism and by reduced levels of public knowledge' (60). A similar position was argued by Natalie Fenton (2013a: 131).

One might contest Curran's research – to question whether a survey of this kind can conclusively demonstrate a connection between a particular level of public knowledge and the influence of the market on the content of the news. Whatever the position taken on its findings, however, the project serves to remind us of the importance of Turow's fundamental question: 'what does society need from the media'? If the media once served the public good as a matter of course, and if they no longer do that, this constitutes a social deficit that should be of concern to a critical media and cultural studies. My purpose here, however, is not to develop *that* critique but rather to raise the question of what has happened to the notion of the public good in the current conjuncture. This is particularly important because that notion was so fundamental to the conception of the media's social and cultural function within the mass media era, and because the media's commitment to serving the public good has been significantly downgraded as the mass media paradigm has undergone the mutations described in the Introduction. This downgrading is by no means confined to the British tabloids or to Fox News; it flows out of the widespread shift from, as it were, a broadcast media paradigm to a narrowcast media paradigm; and it constitutes a major change not only in the media's social function but also in the media industries' understanding of themselves and of the interests they serve.

There is a further angle of inspection onto all of this, which has to do with the changing status of information as well as of the media that circulate it. Among the consequences of the shift from information to entertainment in the news media has been a loss of authority not only for the news media but also in news itself, and even more alarmingly in the validity of empirical information. In particular, as the news media have begun to invest more heavily in comment and opinion as a means of constructing the identity of their brands within a crowded market, the traditional (and important) distinction between reporting and commentary has begun to dissolve. Ironically, notwithstanding the decline in the status of news and despite the exorbitance of the investment in opinion, there is still some residual 'reality effect' (Hall, 1982: 75) available to these commentators as a result of their use of the platforms and discourses identified with the news. This can be quite shamelessly exploited. There are plenty of instances where inaccurate, discredited, but vehemently expressed claims have been treated by media organisations as if they were, nonetheless, true (the belief of the 'birthers' that Barack Obama is not a US citizen is an example of this). The explicitly partisan nature of these opinions serves to specify an audience by relaying this audience's sentiments, which has the recursive effect of reinforcing their endorsement of the views expressed. Similar to what Stephen Colbert has described as 'truthiness' and what Mark Andrejevic, after Brian Massumi, has described as 'affective facts' (Andrejevic, 2013: 137), these claims are *felt* to be true because of the affective investment in them: the anger, resentment, indignation and other emotions that flow from the audience's social, political or cultural identification. As a result, Andrejevic says, now the news can be 'marketed as branded entertainment that relies on emotional engagement' (48).

Andrejevic also points to the role 'played by the background understanding on the part of viewers that facts, information and news have become a matter of choice, faith, or contingent commitment' (49). Rather than a context in which the nightly broadcast news circulated a validated body of information that provided the basis for a public consensus on 'the way it is' at the moment, what Sunstein (2009) describes as the 'balkanisation' of news divides the audience into self-selecting fragments, thereby dramatically increasing the social and political significance of personal choice. The readiness to choose and customise one's news, Andrejevic (2013) argues, 'depends not just on the multiplication of available choices, but also on a reconceptualization of news as a customizable commodity subject to the vagaries of taste that govern other forms of consumption' (49). The commodification of the news, its transformation into entertainment, relativises its ontological status. If it is a commodity, then it doesn't have to be true; it just has to be perceived as having value. In such a context, any attempt to insist upon the validity of empirical information that runs against the grain of what the audience already believes – such as an 'expert' opinion – is likely to be dismissed as the expression of the 'elite' and thus not to be trusted. There is a class dimension to this, of course, as Andrejevic points out in relation to the 'populist logic' of Fox News. There, he continues, the tendency is to vigorously 'debunk the proposition of an empirical fact', 'as if it was an (elitist) attack' on the audience's 'affective attachment'; this amounts to an assault on their taste (60).

As Andrejevic concedes, there is nothing particularly new about people dismissing evidence 'that does not accord with their commitments and beliefs'. However, now, he argues, 'such practices are mainstreamed in the form of a savvy critique of representation associated with a reflexive culture of information abundance'; paradoxically, the amount of information available actually serves to devalue the status of information itself. Andrejevic describes an 'interlocking relationship' between what he calls the advent of 'information glut', the Zizek notion of the 'demise of symbolic efficiency' (that is, the existence of a generally accepted standard, not of truth, but of that which might be understood to legitimise or guarantee it), and a 'renewed focus on the role of affect and emotion as alternative modalities for thinking about the role of communication in a post-referential era' (139). The glut in the supply of information undermines the facticity of that information, thus expanding the choices available to the consumer as they calibrate the level of credibility they wish to give to the information. The operation of those choices is driven as much by affect as by any other form of rationalisation. Viewed from the perspective of this shift, the traditional distinction between news and entertainment seems to have become irrelevant.

The commodification of information and the 'culture of search'

If the news media have withdrawn, or are in the process of withdrawing, from their responsibilities to the public interest, it is worth asking if, and to what extent, that gap has been filled by the avalanche of data that is now available to the individual consumer at the click of a mouse? We can start by recognising just how substantial a shift this new world of information represents, not only in what the media does, but in what *we* do with what the media does. Hillis *et al.* (2013) ask rhetorically, 'what did you do before Google?' (1), as a way of demonstrating how thoroughly naturalised the practice of searching the web for information has become – from the 'life-altering to the trivial'. In the US, search is the most performed internet activity; 'in July 2011 alone', Hillis *et al.* report, 'Americans conducted 19.2 billion core search queries' (3), and presumably the current count would be much higher. Indeed, they argue that the 'culture of search' has become 'a way of life' (4); presumably a deliberately hyperbolic claim, it nonetheless serves to highlight the extent to which search has been integrated into the ways of life of many consumers around the globe. In highly developed consumerist countries, it has transformed the sales and purchase practices employed by retailers and shoppers, and for those employed in information-based professions such as journalism, it has transformed their working lives.

Google is much easier to use than a library but, unlike the library, the cultural capital required to access and use it, in highly technologised societies, is both minimal and diminishing. Google's availability across devices, mobile and fixed, extends its reach across all sectors of society and around the globe – into, for instance, societies where computer ownership is not widespread, where locations are impermanent, and where the mobile or cellphone is the primary means of accessing the web. Its ubiquity alone does not make it a democratising technology, of course, but it matters that its capabilities are available in places, and to users, that had been without such capabilities before. Among the benefits it delivers is access to news and information.

In mainland China, with its centrally controlled media environment, the dissemination of news and opinion through micro-blogs on Weibo has significantly expanded the range of independent inputs into the public sphere, thus giving the population access to information that would otherwise have been suppressed or restricted, rather than publicly available. While online activity is monitored and controlled in China, the use of external IP addresses and other methods has resulted in the creation of so-called 'netizens', who are using their capacity to access non-authorised information as a means of informing themselves, as well as their own networks and publics, about the political conditions in which they live. Whereas in the West, blogs and micro-blogs are overwhelmingly populated through the remediation of news and information from their mainstream media, in China it has worked the other way round. Journalists who are unable to publish information through their conventional media outlets have made use of blogging and micro-blogging as a means of getting the information into the public domain, where it can then be picked up and reported in the mainstream media outlets. This may well remind us of the practices of the elite cadre of media professionals who dominate the blogosphere in the West (Hindman, 2009), but the politics of the Chinese activities are not necessarily the same. While the complexities of the Chinese context are numerous and I am not at all suggesting this constitutes a major reconfiguration of political power there, any significant expansion of the public sphere – for entertainment as much as for information – must be a net benefit.

Retrieving information at will is one of the things that virtually everyone, who can, now does with the media. However, the extent to which this capacity, of itself, constitutes a form of democratisation now seems extremely limited (Turner, 2010: 126–133). Expectations in the West that user-generated news content – from citizen journalists and bloggers, for instance – would dramatically increase the supply of information have not been met. Traditional media are still overwhelmingly the major sources of news reporting with user-generated activity dominated by remediation and commentary or opinion (Lovink, 2013; Hindman, 2009). A core argument against the digital optimists' claims for the democratisation of the media was that the symbolic economy was always likely to remain in the hands of those who currently controlled it – rather than those 'formerly known as the audience' (Rosen, 2006) – because that was where the commercial power was currently located (Turner, 2010). The development of the digital infrastructure for the online environment – given its alignment with small-scale entrepreneurs, grassroots start-ups, the mythology of the long tail, and thus the projection of a redistribution of commercial power – was nonetheless thought to presage a very different future.

As the digital behemoths such as Google, Amazon and Facebook have gradually emerged, absorbing smaller entities as they grow, the chances of such a future actually eventuating look slim. As David Morley (2007) has noted (drawing on Des Freedman), over a relatively short period the internet has mutated from being mainly a 'non-commercial instrument of information exchange into a highly commercialised tool of mainly private and business transactions'. Technological developments, Morley goes on, 'have played only a minor role' in this process (Morley, 2007: 241); the major players have been corporations and governments.

Although Google is one of these digital behemoths, Hillis *et al.* (2013) argue that it also has a legitimate claim to be seen as an organisation that has more than commercial objectives in its sights. Indeed, one could argue that Google is more convincingly committed to serving the public good than some of the news organisations mentioned in the previous section of the chapter. Admittedly, Wikipedia would be a much better example of an online organisation that has maintained an unambiguous commitment to serving the public good,[2] but Google is especially interesting not only for its power and ubiquity but also for its ideological hybridity. Hillis *et al.* note Google's imbrication in what they call the 'Californian ideology' (48) that motivated the entrepreneurs behind so much of the commercial development of connective media. This is the contradiction I discussed in the Introduction: the conflict between a progressive libertarianism and a free market capitalism that generates the political ambiguity of connective media as it simultaneously supports the dual capacities of empowerment and exploitation. Hillis *et al.* argue, convincingly I think, that

> despite the growing pressures of commercialisation within the field of search, Google has negotiated a path that allows it to maintain some of the idealistic qualities associated with the early search industry and which continue to inform the broader social and cultural forces shaping the Web's commercialisation.
> (Hillis *et al.*, 2013: 35)

In fact, the public good is one of the values implicitly (if perhaps disingenuously) embedded in the ideological equation Hillis *et al.* suggest underwrites the Google enterprise, and constitutes its attraction for many of its users: the framing relationship to the trope of 'democracy-as-connection through technology-as-progress' (201). As a result, the authors argue, Google, while still a private firm and a virtual monopoly, is nonetheless 'widely perceived as a trustworthy institutional provider of a public good within a networked society that has elevated total information awareness to the status of first principle' (200). Indeed, it is because Google has been able to build 'the consumer trust and legitimacy that allows it to accumulate' both 'economic *and* cultural capital' that its industry dominance has been so wholeheartedly 'consecrated' (46).

Nonetheless, there is still the other side to the story: the issues of personal privacy and security, the implications of Google's gradual institutional transition from providing 'managed support for consumer "discovery" to managed "data recovery"' (37), as well as the fact that Google has been 'profoundly shaped by the field of advertising' (38). There is also the issue that has attracted an increasing amount of attention as time has gone on – the social and political roles played by what we no longer accept as innocent and value-free modes of organising the culture of search, the search algorithms:

> It is humans who design these entities which can seem to take on lives of their own. Search algorithm coding, however, reflects the dispositions, the habitus, the assumptions of its coders. They operate within fields of engineering and technology development and diffusion that are in direct encounter with free market, libertarian, autocratic, democratic, utopian and globalizing ideologies. One such disposition designed into these machines … is the West's progressive interest in automating the quest for enlightenment through technology … Easy, efficient, rapid, and total access to Truth is the siren song of Google and the culture of search. (5)

Apart from the stealthily ideological operation of these codes, what is most alarming about the rise of the algorithm is that most of us don't understand them. As Andrejevic (2013: 18) points out, there is a serious knowledge asymmetry here: 'the divide between those who generate the data and those who put it to use by turning it back on the population'. This divide is not only to do with our (lack of) knowledge about the infrastructure, but it is also epistemological: 'a difference in forms of practical knowledge available to those with access to the database, in the way they think about and use information' (ibid.). This is not a divide which is easily bridged.

At the moment, it makes sense to see the culture of search as one in which there is a complex mixture of gains and losses for the ordinary person. The access to an expanded field of information is clearly a substantial gain, but the manner in which that access is operated – Google's end of the culture of search – is subject to control and direction that in the end must serve the commercial interests of the organisation rather than those of the consumer. The indications are that this is only going to become more so in the future. In the first instance, of course, this was aimed at rendering the results of search more coherent for the consumer and better targeted for the advertiser – both parties seeking a means of dealing with the sheer volume of the information available. As time went by, however, consumers have sought some means of further tailoring that process. This is particularly the case when the preferred means of engaging with the internet is via mobile devices but there is also the more general issue of what has been described in relation to television as 'choice fatigue' (Ellis, 2002). As advertisers respond to this desire, the culture of search, especially as utilised via mobile devices, is gradually mutating into a culture of 'apps' – of tailored applications aimed at making use of a much more narrow set of parameters in order to search for designated categories of content. Since apps provide a 'more structured form of targeting and customization', many media companies have begun to 'utilise their apps rather than their websites to push their best and most timely content', and comScore has reported that 'during a three month period ending in November 2011, mobile users said they used apps more often than web browsers' (Lee and Andrejevic, 2014: 45).

While apps offer more directed access and thus carry the benefits of salience and convenience for the consumer, their growing prevalence results in the online environment becoming 'more of a closed system with limited and directed functionality' that is more tightly articulated to commercial interests (Tussey, 2014: 210). Manovich's (2008) model of the online environment functioning as an open database is giving way to something that looks more like a supermarket or, maybe, a department store. The logic of this is by now entirely familiar. Lee and Andrejevic (2014) remind us of Jonathan Zittrain's prediction, from 2008, that 'as computers become more applianciced and tethered to marketers' desires, the internet will become less about user creativity than about structured consumption and marketing opportunities'. While they have reservations about the terms of this opposition (and, indeed, they point out that the internet has 'never really been free, open and uncontrolled'), they agree that this is more or less what has happened as the internet has gone from being 'a technology of creative participation to one of consumption, commerce and entertainment' (45).

If one thinks, however, about what is still offered by the culture of search, notwithstanding the steady progress towards its enclosure and commercialisation, there are a couple of points to make. First, there is a sense in which search, more than any other aspect of the contemporary media, may constitute the most genuine location for those Reithian desires: that the media should inform, educate and entertain. Search connects us to all of these capacities in abundance. Unlike most of the rest of the media, however, it tends not to be interested in distinguishing between them. When one searches for a favourite song on Google, in the first page of results will be a link to YouTube. Once there, down the right hand side of your screen you will not only find a number of performances of the song but also interviews with the musician and then perhaps links to instruction videos on how to play the song on your guitar. In such a case, the lines between education, information and entertainment blur in an ongoing and contingent process of hybridisation. Second, while the benefits of being able to access more detail and more sources on your chosen news story should not be discounted, the problem for the future is that so much of this information is derived from news media where the independent production of information is in decline. Consequently, the capacity for search to compensate for the shift from news to entertainment by providing alternative sources of content is extremely limited. Search retrieves, aggregates, curates and manages information; by and large, and notwithstanding the promises of the blogosphere, it does little to produce it.

Information, moreover, is not what it used to be. Abundant though it is today, it doesn't work the same way for the re-invented media as it did for the traditional media. For a start, the scale of the information available actually limits our capacity to benefit from it. Andrejevic's (2013) *Infoglut* describes a situation where citizens are faced with what he describes as 'an unimaginably unmanageable flow of mediated information' that is readily available to anyone with internet access. The task of sorting it out properly is beyond us: 'at the very moment when we have the technology available to inform ourselves as never before, we are simultaneously and compellingly confronted with the impossibility of ever being *fully* informed' (2). What makes this paradox particularly disturbing, Andrejevic goes on, is that this is occurring at 'the very moment when we are told that being informed is more important than ever before to our livelihood, our security and our social lives' (ibid.). Finding ways of 'cutting through the clutter' (ibid.) has led governments, corporations, institutions, all kinds of organisations and enterprises, to develop automated strategies such as data-mining, predictive analytics, sentiment analysis or body language analysis to assist them in organising the mass of data they collect, or to which they have access. These strategies are 'shortcuts' designed to 'bypass the need to comprehend proliferating narrative or referential representations' (4), in favour of other principles of analysis. As a result, there is a sense in which these shortcuts operate as more or less compromised proxies for modes of understanding we might have preferred to deploy when faced with more manageable bodies of information. The online enterprises managing this information have moved away from an advertiser-funded model and towards a primary strategy of monetising the by-products of consumers' engagement with their sites, 'the exploitation of user data' (Lovink, 2013: 13). As a result, the flow of information now goes both ways: in order for consumers to access the information they seek, they must provide commercial entities with access to their personal details, which are then commodified and sold to third parties.

As we engage in drawing up the political balance sheet on this aspect of the re-invention of the media, we are entitled to ask just who turns out to have benefited from this new world of information. The strategies developed to deal with 'infoglut' have evolved into new strategies of management and control that have been taken up within the realms of politics, finance, marketing, security and more. The scale of this take-up reflects one of the fundamental features of this reconfigured world of information: the power accruing to those who possess the data and to those who control the means of controlling data, of managing the means through which ordinary people are enabled to make sense of information. That power is highly concentrated, in various ways, rather than widely or equitably dispersed. As a result, the commodification of personal information that has come to be labelled data-mining is emerging as one of the more worrying outcomes of the rise of interactive media: issues around privacy, around the protocols for consent, around the lack of transparency surrounding these protocols, and about the sustainability of the concept of privacy itself have been raised at some length by Andrejevic (2013), Sunstein (2009) and many others.

Joseph Turow's (2011) *The Daily You* is focused in particular on the US advertising industry, the key user of the data mined from the details consumers submit online. Once fundamentally oriented towards mass marketing, the contemporary advertising industry increasingly targets the individual with the aid of data generated online as well as many other kinds of monitoring and surveillance instruments – such as the loyalty programmes in supermarkets, airlines and hotels, for instance. Turow analyses the changes to this industry, as it seeks to target 'particular types of individuals – and, increasingly, *particular* individuals – by leveraging a detailed knowledge about them and their behaviours that were unheard of even a few years ago' (Turow, 2011: 4). While acknowledging that 'there are many great things about the new media environment', Turow raises the alarm about the likely social consequences of some things that are *not* so great: 'when companies track people without their knowledge, sell their data without letting them know what they are doing or securing their permission, and then use those data to decide which of those people are targets or waste, we have a serious social problem' (8). He admits that while the 'precise implications of this problem are not yet clear' there is still reason for concern:

> If it is allowed to persist, and people begin to realise how the advertising industry segregates them from and pits them against others in the ads they get, the discounts they receive, the TV-viewing suggestions and news stories they confront, and even the offers they receive in the supermarket, they may begin to suffer the effects of discrimination. They will likely learn to distrust the companies that have put them in this situation, and they may well be incensed at the government that has not helped to prevent it. A comparison to the financial industry is apt. Here was an industry engaged in a whole spectrum of arcane practices that were not at all transparent to consumers or regulators but that had serious negative impact on our lives. It would be deeply unfortunate if the advertising system followed the same trajectory. (8)

As noted in the previous chapter, there are claims that consumers are, to some extent and in the short term, aware of the fact that their data is commodified, but that they are prepared to see this as an acceptable trade-off for the customisation and personalisation that flows from their participation in the relevant site, network or commercial transaction. Turow suggests that this is something of a myth as well. Revisiting Negroponte's (1995) optimistic scenarios for the future personalisation and customisation of information, Turow points out that, in fact, much of this content is not customised and personalised by consumers themselves. Rather, advertisements, discounts, information and entertainment are customised by a largely invisible industry on the basis of the information it has already collected about individual consumers without their consent or knowledge.

Conclusion

What this chapter has set out to do is map some of the key changes that have taken place in the provision and management of information as the media has re-invented itself. In terms of my initial focus on the mutation of the mission of news and current affairs, it seems to me that the trends are clear. By and large, and this probably reflects the extent of the globalisation of the major news media, they also seem to me to be significantly transnational. There are lots of differences and nuances, of course, as we move from location to location, but in general the news media does seem to me to have engaged in a process of redefinition around the centrality of entertainment. Even in those sectors of the news media that have not yet been privatised or commercialised, this trend is evident.[3] What is also evident is that the news media has itself revised its thinking about its social and cultural function as it accommodates itself to the current operating environment (and we will return to that point in Chapter 5). In particular, the idea that the news media should serve the public good, a residue of the original rationale for both public and private investment in the development of the infrastructure for the mass media, no longer automatically commands assent.

The chapter then asks whether the expansion in the provision of information online compensates for the diminution of the importance of the public good in news and current affairs. While the points of access to news have multiplied, the quantum amount of news on offer has probably not shifted all that much – especially when we consider the effect of the slow decline of the print media in many markets and the gradual displacement of conventional news with entertainment content. What does the culture of search have to offer instead? Without understating the positive value of our expanded access to information online, it is hard not to notice that the potential benefits of open access to information are shrinking as the internet is captured by the market. The development of a whole new industry of applications to manage and streamline our searching online is, in many ways, a sign that the ideal of an open, community-oriented, internet is not likely to be maintained for long in the face of the commodification of information. This is further complicated by what must now be a familiar dialectic in our discussion of the politics of the internet: that is, the contradictory potentials of empowerment and exploitation (Banet-Weiser, 2012). We are finding that while the capacities provided by these technologies are potentially transformative, their commodification almost inevitably turns them in the direction of private profit rather than the public good. This does not deny their productivity for those who use them, but it does incline us towards a particular view of their social function.

There may be no conclusive answer to my question – does access to information online compensate for the degrading of the information provided by the news media? But one would have to say that the digital environment hasn't turned out to be nearly as 'empowering' as its early enthusiasts had hoped. I would actually prefer to dispense with the term 'empowerment' altogether in this context as, in my view, it fundamentally overstates what is realistically possible within the current configurations of power. I am drawn to a comment from Sarah Bunting, the creator of the Television Without Pity site, quoted in Sharon Ross's *Beyond the Box*. Describing how fan communities had formed around particular television shows, Bunting says she prefers to describe the fans she deals with as 'emboldened', rather than 'empowered':

> The Internet really allowed these communities to come together and allowed people to feel – I hate the word 'empowered', so – 'emboldened' to sort of lay claim to their fandom of certain shows. Not so much that they got to dictate

what happened on the shows – it was much more about this feeling that you were not alone. (Ross, 2008: 232)

I find that a useful way of describing what is going on here. At the level of consumption, one has to acknowledge that, in many respects, the capacity for choice has dramatically expanded and there is every reason why that should feel good to those who benefit from it. However, that is at the micro-level of what each consumer might think as they engage with content on their television, their computer or some other device. It looks very different once we widen the frame to consider the regimes of production and, from there, the broader fields of power within which that consumer and those producers are situated. On the one hand, it is tempting to say that within these fields of power, very little has changed; on the other hand, there are also those who argue that there has indeed been significant change and it is not for the better.

Mark Andrejevic, for one, is very clear about what he thinks has changed; he presents an account of 'a reconfiguration of the relationship between forms of knowledge and power' in which two aspects are singled out for particular concern:

> first, the increasing asymmetry between those who are able to capture, store, access, and process the tremendous amount of data produced by the proliferation of digital, interactive sensors of all kinds; and, second, ways of understanding and using information that are uniquely available to those with access to the database. (Andrejevic, 2013: 17)

Andrejevic alludes to the dystopian possibility of a world where control over information is 'concentrated in the hands of the few who use it to sort, manage and manipulate' (ibid.). Given the history of how media power has been distributed and used, and given the steady concentration of media and communications infrastructure around the world – notwithstanding the grassroots potential of the capacities of the digital – this is not at all an unlikely scenario. While I do think that a great deal has changed in terms of the platforms, devices, affordances and choices available via the re-invented media, there is little about the way these changes have played out to support the proposition that they will lead to a re-distribution of power.

What might we conclude from our discussion, so far, about the changing social function of the media? In relation to the areas we have examined in this chapter, I would contend that there has been a significant break with the conception of the media that prevailed in the era of mass media. In the areas we have looked at here, the contemporary media are more thoroughly focused on their commercial interests than the public interest, and that has resulted in a concentration on targeting individual consumers rather than on constructing a community. When we move into other areas of activity, for instance in the next chapter which deals with the media and the state, we will look at some examples from which we might draw quite different implications, so my conclusions here are not meant to be categoric. However, at this point in our investigation, in terms of constructing a calculus of gains and losses in relation to the rise of entertainment and the decline of information in the news media, to the provision of information online and the management of its commodification, and the socio-cultural function of the culture of search, the balance sheet is, in the end, leaning towards a deficit. This is largely due to the reduction of the news media's commitment to the public good which significantly affects the media's social and political role, a role that has always been seen as fundamental to the proper functioning of a democracy, and without introducing an alternative to fill its place.

Notes

1 I am indebted to Mark Andrejevic for making this point to me.
2 José van Dijck (2013) provides an excellent analysis of these issues in her account of the history and development of Wikipedia.
3 I am thinking here of major public broadcasters such as the BBC, where the logics of the market have also had a significant impact on programming, and on shifts in the manner through which the legitimacy of their role is framed, or indeed challenged, by government. A similar story could be told about the ABC (the Australian Broadcasting Corporation), which is continually under attack by those who would rather abandon the idea of a public broadcaster; one of the avenues of defence for the public broadcaster in this situation is to demonstrate community support in the form of audience ratings figures – hence to behave in much the same way as a commercial broadcaster.

PART II

The media and the nation-state

3

THE MEDIA, THE NATION AND GLOBALISATION

The project of rethinking media theory demands explicit attention to the relation between the media and the state in the context of globalisation – simply because, in my view, some of the orthodox treatments of this relation are in need of revision. Fortunately, we seem to have arrived at a moment when that seems possible. Consequently, this chapter responds to what I suggest is a relatively recent shift in the orthodox attitude within media and cultural studies to the contemporary relevance of the nation-state – a shift that has the benefit of opening the way to a more detailed and instantiated examination of the media's relation to the state in the present conjuncture. In contrast to some earlier approaches which overly emphasised the homogenising forces of globalisation, and within which as a consequence the nation-state seemed more or less irrelevant, there is now a strengthening acceptance of the need to recognise and interrogate the diversity of media systems around the world by, among other strategies, returning to a closer analysis of the operating environment established for the media by the nation-state. Importantly, and in accord with the long-running project of 'de-Westernising' media studies (Curran and Park, 2000), the broadening of the range of national environments examined by Anglophone scholars these days – with comparative work extending beyond the core territories for media and cultural studies in English (largely, the UK and the US) – has served to highlight the political, historical, economic and cultural contingency of these environments. In particular, and as a contribution to such a project, this chapter argues for greater attention to the media's imbrication within national projects of modernisation, as an important strategy for understanding the variations in the contemporary relationships between the media and the state. This is particularly useful when we focus upon those nation-states in Asia, in Central Europe, in Africa or in Latin America which are engaged in significant political and/or economic transition. Typically, at the moment, this tends to be a transition towards a marketised and globalising economy or, less often, towards a more liberal polity. How this plays out can vary significantly from place to place but, as I will argue later in the chapter, an analytic approach too closely aligned with the homogenising versions of globalisation inevitably tends to smooth over such differences or, worse, to render them invisible.

In this chapter I suggest, then, that a key feature of the re-invention of the media over the last several decades is an ongoing restructuring of the power relations between the media and the state. All the elements of change we have encountered already – the media's commercialisation, the decline of the mass media paradigm the development of the digital environment – are contributing to this restructuring, but always in contingent and located ways. The examples outlined in the following section are there to highlight that element of contingency.

Television and the nation-state

My starting point in this first section of the chapter is the relation between television and the nation-state, rather than the media more generally – although I will return to this broader picture later in the chapter. In this section I will draw directly on original research which has been generated primarily from within television studies, and to a lesser extent from discussions of digital media, where the orthodoxy to which I refer above has been particularly strong. Indeed, partly as consequence of the close historical, industrial and political connection between broadcast television systems and the nation-state, those working in television studies in the post-broadcast era have repeatedly been warned of the impending demise of both the nation-state *and* television (Katz and Scannell, 2009). In addition, the excitement over media convergence (Jenkins, 2006; Flew, 2007) led to propositions regarding the emergence of a new level of structural autonomy for digital media platforms – which also carried implications for the power of the nation-state over the media, as well as for the future of television. However, and as argued earlier in this book, much of this excitement has proven premature – for the political potential of digital media, for the projected death of television and for the imagined diminution of the relevance of the nation-state. As the nation-state has gradually returned to the mainstream of academic discussions of the media, and particularly of television (Mihelj, 2011; Flew, Iosifidis and Steemers, 2015), we have learned that the character of the relations between the media and the state that now obtain have in some cases transformed significantly and not necessarily in the ways we might have expected (Kaneva, 2012; Voltmer, 2013).

To backtrack a little, however, I should acknowledge that over the last decade or two there have been numerous provocations which led many in television studies towards the conclusion that the nation-state was no longer an especially useful context within which to locate the study of television. The provocations I have in mind – and we have encountered all of these earlier on in this book so I will just list them quickly here – include the decline of central broadcasting institutions and networks in some nation-states, or their conversion from public to private ownership as a means of commercialising their operations; the fragmentation of national, mass, audiences as choices in networks, platforms, channels and programmes proliferate; the expanded trade in television formats that are transnational in terms of their markets although often carefully indigenised in terms of their actual content; and the increasing difficulty in defining what actually constitutes 'national television' (indeed, what constitutes 'television') in the era of transnational online video aggregators such as YouTube, online streaming of network and other television via Hulu, Netflix and the like, as well as the migration of television content from all kinds of sources onto the mobile screens of the smart phone. All of these seriously complicate the once standard model of a central national broadcast television system gathering the attention of a 'convergent audience' (Dayan, 2009: 24) that was addressed as consumers by advertisers and as national citizens by programmers and regulators. This singular model has been replaced by a complex of hybridised and often localised models of television that are riddled with contradictions. Television (however it is defined) is still largely national in its institutional and industrial location, while increasingly transnational in its commercial disinterest in national borders; television is commercially targeted in its address to particular taste cultures, but it is also readily personalised as users take advantage of a range of strategies to enable them to consume customised menus of favourites; and television still addresses a mass audience much of the time, even though a great deal of its content is time-shifted out of schedule, or consumed via DVDs or downloads, without necessarily incorporating much sense of a larger, national, co-presence.

Some observers have opted to emphasise just one side of these contradictions in order to argue that television could no longer function as a means of constructing located imagined communities, that the concept of the national audience was a relic of 'legacy' media, and that television, if it was to survive at all, was heading for a definitively transnational and place-less future. Jean Chalaby suggested that television programmes were now 'deterritorialized artifacts' which 'tear apart the relation between place and television' (Chalaby, 2005: 8), while Ulrich Beck described 'nation-based analysis' of television as a 'zombie category' (cited in Oren, 2012: 373). In some quarters this tendency was welcomed, especially by those who saw the nation-state as an inherently regressive and exclusivist political formation. The emerging transnational alternatives were, it was argued, intrinsically more inclusive and democratic. This argument was driven by the belief that television's institutional disarticulation from the state, together with its enhanced provision of choice and modes of access, would prove to be politically empowering for ordinary people. Not only was such a position connected to the post-modernist distrust of the national as a category (Morley, 2007), as well as (it has to be said) the naïve assumption of an equivalence between market choice and political power, but there was also the more specific factor of the widespread take-up of narratives linking media convergence, globalisation and modernisation (Jenkins, 2006). As time has gone by, and as argued earlier, the 'myth of digital democracy' has been largely discredited (Hindman, 2009), the projected political outcomes have failed to materialise (Lovink, 2013; van Djik, 2013), and there has been a greater acknowledgement of the implicitly 'Westocentric' (Mihelj, 2011: 45) nature of its founding assumptions; that is, it was built upon the normatisation of the consumption practices of highly mediatised and wealthy Western nations. Accounts which focus their analysis on different groups of nation-states (in Central Europe and Latin America, for instance), such as Katrin Voltmer's (2013) study of the media in 'transitional democracies', highlight the fact that it is far from guaranteed that an expanding and commercialising media will result in greater empowerment for ordinary people, or in a more democratic polity (and we will return to that issue in the following chapter).

Other commentators have been more circumspect in their assessment of the evolving role of the nation-state, in one case choosing instead to suggest that the 'global–local dyad' is due for reconsideration, leading to a mode of analysis that is focused on 'regionally bounded, globally linked, locally inflected interactions between nation states and their policies, media tycoons, social actors and media markets' (Kraidy, 2014: 47). Still more argue that while it is no longer appropriate for television studies to only focus on the nation, neither is it helpful to exaggerate the influence of the other factors in play. Representative of such a position is this comment from Tasha Oren, made in relation to the international trade in television formats:

> Arguments that insist on a break or opposition between national experience and global or transnational consciousness conflate the former with state-powered nationalism from above, and sweepingly ascribe chauvinistic and insular disposition to various articulations of national linkages that may operate quite differently, ignoring currently occurring multiplicities that *necessarily* make up the national experience of viewing. More importantly, they cut off the possibility of national address as itself part of the meaning viewers make of transnational media texts. Here I suggest the international format as one such textual category where the national frame comes into view precisely *because* and *within* the understanding of such programming as multi-national reiterations. (Oren, 2012: 374)

Oren is among the increasing number of television studies researchers now presenting evidence that usefully qualifies and complicates the more universalising claims made for the future trajectory of television by, among other things, reclaiming the need to properly examine the significance of the role of the nation within the context of media convergence and globalisation. Sabina Mihelj's (2011) *Media Nations* goes a little further, reasserting the continuing cultural centrality of our identification with the nation: 'outside of the narrow circle of cosmopolitan elites and diasporic communities' she says, 'whose allegiances span across several countries, being a member of a nation – and normally one single nation – is still seen as an indispensable attribute of humanity' (1). And Joseph Straubhaar's take on the relation between the global and the national resists attributing to the former the overdetermining power that Beck and others do. For Straubhaar, globalisation is simply another 'new layer' of 'meaning, culture, identity and media use'; while 'recent layers are important', he says, it is also important to acknowledge that they are actually built up 'over older layers, which are still there' (Straubhaar, 2014:11).

While the numbers of researchers announcing the death of television and the nation-state have fallen dramatically over the last five years, then (as noted in Amanda Lotz's revised edition of *The Television will be Revolutionized* [Lotz, 2014a: xiii]), the comments cited from Beck and others indicate that there is nevertheless a significant body of opinion that needs to be contested if we are to properly understand television in the current era. My own research over the last decade has focused upon contributing to such a project, and I want to draw on it here in order to argue that television studies first, and media and communications studies more generally, far from accepting glib dismissals of nation-based analysis as a 'zombie category', need to recognise the necessity of better understanding the diversity and contingency of the relation between television and the nation around the globe. It can do this by, in turn, recognising the importance of the specific conditions – historical, political, economic, geo-linguistic and cultural – under which that relation has developed in each case.[1]

The research to which I refer here was a large international comparative and collaborative study that examined the roles of television and, to a lesser extent, of new media in the construction of national communities in the post-broadcast era. Among the nation-states and regional markets examined, in addition to some of the usual Anglophone markets (the US, the UK and Australia), were India, some of the Chinese language markets in Asia (Singapore, China, Hong Kong and Taiwan) and a key market within Latin America (Mexico). I worked in collaboration with an interdisciplinary team of researchers possessed of the relevant language skills and cultural competencies for these markets. Those working on this project in the non-Anglo contexts were Anna Cristina Pertierra (Mexico), Jinna Tay (China, Hong Kong, Singapore, Taiwan) and Sukhmani Khorana (India). Outcomes from the project have been published in, among other locations, *Locating Television* (Pertierra and Turner, 2013), *Television Studies after TV* (Turner and Tay, 2009), and a special issue of *Media International Australia* (August, 2014) devoted to the public sphere and the media in India, co-edited by Sukhmani Khorana, Vibodh Parthasarathi, and Pradip Thomas (Khorana *et al.*, 2014).

While this was not initially our objective, the research we conducted led us towards conclusions which reconfirmed the continuing importance of the nation-state as the location through which the media mostly addressed their audiences, as the key influence on the structure of the operating environments for the media industries, and as a continuing political rationale for the development of communications and media infrastructure. Even though our research also reconfirmed Michael Curtin's (2004) observation that it is no longer *sufficient* to examine the media through its relation to the nation-state, we concluded that neither, most of the time, can it be avoided. Far from being irrelevant, the role of the nation was pervasive and, given a degree of flexibility that may not have been foreseen, arguably just as capable of regaining as of losing influence. Among the particular aspects of this role that we noticed in the locations we examined – and some of these have been noted by researchers speaking from other locations as well (Dhoest, 2013; Freedman, 2015; Meikle and Young, 2012) – were the resilience and continuing viability of some national broadcasters in response to competition from subscription TV and other platforms; the persistence of the national audience even in contexts where there were no supportive cultural policy settings or even much in the way of a nationalist discourse around television production; and evidence from non-democratic countries that, in such political environments, there is little that is inherently difficult about regulating the internet in alignment with the nation-state's political interests.

I work in Australia, where the nation-state has always played a significant regulatory and subventionary role in the media and communications industries: subsidising the production of local content, regulating and licensing participants in the media industries, and setting up self-regulatory environments in the relative simplicity of a remote geographic location. After a burst of deregulation over the last decade and a half, there has recently been an attempt to establish a comprehensive cross-media regulatory regime that would deal with television, print, radio and online media all together. That attempt failed – largely due to the resistance from a print media that wanted to retain its existing regulator because it had been thoroughly captured by those it was meant to regulate. However, if you place that initiative together with the establishment of the Leveson inquiry in the UK and the slow parade of News International's phone-hackers through the British courts, it does suggest that in these two countries at least there is something of a revival of the state's interest in regulating the behaviour of the national media in order to manage its performance against community standards and/or notions of the public good. Perhaps this has always been a default, though dormant, setting in both contexts, ready to be activated when a specific threat appeared – such as the tabloid excesses produced by a hypercompetitive commercial media or the activities of a powerful transnational media proprietor. However, in both countries, the state has experienced considerable difficulty in exercising its power to influence the media's behaviour, even though, in both cases, it had the legal and regulatory authority to do so. The state had earlier on, under the influence of a deregulatory politics, walked away from that policy domain, thus creating the problem they encountered when they sought to reactivate their interest.

In contrast, when we head towards the fringes of the customary locations for the discussion of the globalisation of the media, that is, beyond the Anglophone nation-states in the West, we find that in many locations the continuing importance and engagement of the nation-state has never been in doubt. As the examples I want to go through briefly now will indicate, the reasons for this can be quite varied – in terms of both their political and their cultural objectives. Furthermore, while the state may have maintained its influence, the nature of its compact with the media generally, and with the television industry in particular, may have undergone some significant changes. These can be mapped through close attention to the manner in which settlements have been struck between the activities and interests of the state, the market, the media, and the national public or community. Each of the three examples that follow – all of them to do with, but resonating beyond, television – articulate their own distinctive arrangement of these elements, and thus a specific configuration of the relation between the media and the state.

In those nation-states where the media has never been framed as an enabling institution for a functioning democracy, but rather is treated as an arm of government and a means of maintaining political control, there is very little political reason for the state to relinquish that control – although there are often internal political reasons for changing how that control is exercised, towards which aspects of the media it will be directed, and how all this is to be publicly represented. As one might expect, the most dramatic examples of the persistence of the state, from among our research sites, come from authoritarian regimes (Singapore, China, Hong Kong), where, even in the context of what is regarded as significant media liberalisation in terms of increased consumer choice or the managed marketisation of the sector, there is little evidence of the state relinquishing its ambition of maintaining political control. In China, so far, the marketisation of the media has largely resulted in the imposition of a layer of commercial objectives on top of the already existing political frameworks for the media's operation, rather than the displacement of the latter by the former. What is interesting about Singapore, however, is its take-up – elsewhere in Asia, in particular, but crucially in China – as an influential political model for incorporating a programme of media liberalisation within a larger process of economic and cultural modernisation. The so-called 'Singapore model' (Chua, 2005, 2011), as it relates to the media, includes the relaxation of restrictions on entertainment content and an expansion of consumer choice, particularly in relation to access to iconic global media formats and brands. This appears to be aimed at reducing the pressure for political change in other, more fundamental, social arenas by satisfying the demands of a rising consumerist middle class. What looks like a withdrawal of the state from closely managing the provision of entertainment demonstrates its commitment to modernisation and to globalisation, while at the same time it operates in such a way as to establish a 'softer' but nonetheless effective regime of state power. As Dahlgren has noted, even while apparently 'opening' the internet, the Chinese government has 'continually managed to increase the level of sophistication in its internal filter powers' in such a way that 'paradoxically, both freedom and control seem to be on the rise' (Dahlgren, 2009: 162). It is hard to argue, therefore, in the case of Singapore and certainly of China, that an apparently increased openness to global markets and a more liberal response to new media environments, including the widening of online access and an expansion of consumer choices for television and mobile entertainment, has in fact 'weakened' the power of the nation-state. Rather, we have the mobilisation of a more strategic understanding of how that power might be localised and exercised even within a liberalising regulatory regime for the media overall.

The second example is a site Anna Pertierra and I initially chose for its significance as a media producer within a transnational geo-linguistic region rather than as a representative of a particular kind of nation-state. As part of the initial aims of our project, we wished to investigate whether the conceptual and structural role of the geo-linguistic region has in any way displaced that of the nation-state. Our research in Mexico (Pertierra and Turner, 2013) tells a story that once again alters the coordinates we might use to map the relation between the media and the state, and challenges our original assumption that their identification with the geo-linguistic region – the

Spanish-speaking nations of Latin America – would actually constitute a significant factor in how our Mexican subjects experienced the consumption of television.

Mexico is a highly mediatised nation-state, with a well-developed and internationally competitive television industry that effectively dominates the Latin American regional market as well as the Hispanic market in the US. Given its success as an exporter of content, there is little need for regulatory protection of the production of local content and so the state has played a minimal policy role in relation to the media. Locally produced television dominates prime-time, although our research found that our Mexican informants tended to assume that anything on their screens which looked like it came from Latin America had been produced in Mexico (Pertierra and Turner, 2013). While *telenovelas* from other Latin American locations were certainly screened and watched enthusiastically, our informants displayed little interest in the national origins of this programming. Rather, there was, in effect, a default national orientation in the consumer's mind, implying the assumption of a strong national co-presence for Mexican audiences as they watched television.

In contrast to the examples of Singapore and China, in both of which locations there was a strong state and a relatively weak media, Mexico is a nation where the state is relatively weak and the media relatively strong. The domestic television market, as well as much of Mexico's participation within the regional television market, is dominated by two commercial networks with close relationships to organised politics and to the state. Indeed, the closeness of the relation between the networks and politics has resulted in corruption scandals; a recent example involved allegations that one of the networks sold favourable coverage to a political candidate in the 2012 election. The leading network, Televisa, has further blurred the boundary between the industry and the state by taking on what is effectively the role of a national cultural institution: among other ventures, it has constructed a museum of modern art and funded a major intellectual journal (Pertierra and Turner, 2013: 53–54). While these certainly constitute a public good, and in many ways offer a highly pro-social example of corporate investment, it is also clear that Televisa's relationship with the state, in the end, has to be dominated by its own interests; that is, developing commercial markets and employing its media power for profit and political influence. In Mexico, while television audiences appear to experience a relatively straightforward discursive identification with the nation, at the structural and political level the state has, more or less, allowed itself to be captured by commercial interests (Voltmer, 2013: 175–176).

In the case of the transformation of the television industry in India, my third example, it might appear as if the nation-state had simply gone away – with the public broadcaster, Doordarshan, relinquishing its longstanding dominance and thus opening the way for commercial and community interests to prevail. However, it may turn out to be a little more complicated than that. The 'age of television' (Athique, 2009) begins fairly recently in India, with a spate of deregulation and local/regional development over the 1990s, as the state-run television service monopoly collapses and the provision of commercial television services explodes, resulting in the establishment of literally hundreds of new channels, many of them broadcasting in languages other than Hindi. As Mihelj notes, this was a highly localised and regionalised development, or as she describes it 'a sub-state diversification', as 'Indian television was turned into a battleground for competing visions of community' (Mihelj, 2011: 42). This, Mihelj continues, drawing on Shanti Kumar, made it 'impossible to talk of a single Indian community of television', and thus demonstrates the capacity of this new media order to generate cultural diversity and to prosecute 'cultural identities that hitherto received little space in the national media system' (ibid.).

This is only one of many arguments one might make about the implications of the radical and multi-faceted expansion of the Indian television environment, however. Sukhmani Khorana's research takes us in a different direction. Khorana examines the gradual articulation of core genres of Indian commercial media content (mostly, news and current affairs television but print media as well) to middle-class versions of national identity which are in turn discursively structured around a particular narrativisation of India's national project of modernisation. Khorana argues that this narrative is implicitly addressed to an international or global audience as a means of redefining and modernising the internationally received idea of India's national identity, and is to be used as an instrument of India's emerging capacity to wield so-called 'soft power' internationally through its media and entertainment industries (Khorana, 2012: 2014).

This might be seen as evidence of the resilience of the nation-state but I would also regard it as a sign of a change in how the nation-state operates these days. In India, Khorana's research suggests, it would seem that the nation-state is less interested in creating a national public than in identifying one sector of the national community as the core element in India's national brand within a global marketplace of commercialised national identities. Consistent with the post-1990s development of nation-branding (Kaneva, 2012), and with the commercial appropriation of established discourses of nationalism that Zala Volcic (2013) has examined in the nation-states emerging from the former Yugoslavia, this seems to be the territory where the narratives of media globalisation and the national project of modernity come into close and productive alignment. Together, they signal what is still a relatively new field of activity for the nation-state as a response to the volatile forces unleashed by the increased transnational interdependencies of global commerce: the strategic branding and commercialisation of national identities for international consumption.

In each of these examples we can see a distinctive configuration of the power relations between the media and the state, all of them different from the models that are most active in the Anglophone West. All of these examples, however, come from television, and in the next section I want to widen the frame and discuss some of these issues in relation to the media more broadly.

Globalisation, the media and modernity

The conference at which an earlier version of some of the arguments in this chapter was presented in 2013[2] directly addressed what it described as the 'return of the state' as an important factor in the consideration of the changing climate for global communications. The intellectual context for this was the currency of the kind of debates about the globalisation of the media I noted earlier in relation to television: those which have tended to conclude that the combination of deregulatory state policies, the capacity for online communications to ignore national borders, the rise of large transnational media organisations, and the expansion in transnational trade in media products, have led to a media environment in which the power and significance of the nation-state has been dramatically reduced. As was the case with the analysis of television, this more broadly framed proposition has not gone uncontested (Mihelj, 2011). Nonetheless, as I noted at the beginning of this chapter, the assumption that the power of the state has declined as we have entered the new order of media and communications has been one of the orthodoxies underpinning a number of influential narratives of media development, particularly in the West, over the last decade or so.

It was somewhat surprising, then, when the presentations at this conference were overwhelmingly critical of this orthodoxy. While not an uncomplicated consensus, the papers presented did reflect a common view that the state had been written off far too early, and that the nation had not only retained its significance but in certain contexts may well have expanded its influence. There was an implicit, and indeed at times explicit, recognition that some earlier versions of the globalisation orthodoxy were too closely tied to the experience of those living and working in the West and the global North, and that this needed to be corrected. The selection of presenters, in effect, addressed this directly; the 36 speakers came from 16 different countries and six continents. As a consequence, the conference provided a dramatic demonstration of the diversity of local, national and regional media systems today, and showed how unwise it is to assume that there might be a single narrative to describe the contemporary conditions for the development of the media around the globe.

The research project discussed in the previous section came to a similar conclusion. We found so much variation in media operating environments among the nations we investigated, and the factors influencing these variations were so diverse, that it was difficult to point to any one complex of factors that we could identify as key components of a process of globalisation. This encouraged scepticism, certainly about the more totalising versions of theories of globalisation, but also perhaps even about the value of the concept itself. Garcia Canclini, while wryly describing globalisation as an 'unidentified cultural object', has expressed his view that there is no 'singular model of development' we might identify in the experience of globalisation; hence his preference for focusing upon globalisation as a 'collective of narratives' (Garcia Canclini, 2014: 26) that inform the imagination:

> If we understand globalisation in the classic sense, such as formulated by Ulrich Beck, as a radical increase in the interdependence of all countries and societies, that interdependence is conceived in very different ways by the managers of corporations, culture industries, documented or undocumented migrants, and people in other professions and of other nationalities. That diversity, quite

visible already at the end of the twentieth century, led me to think of globalisation as something partly imagined. (203)

Garcia Canclini provides examples of the specific forms of these imaginaries, which depend on who you are, or where you are, or what your status might be:

> How we imagine globalization varies: for the CEOs of transnational corporations, *globalization* principally encompasses the countries where their businesses operate, the activities they engage in, and competition with other companies; for Latin American rulers who focus on trade with the United States, globalization is almost synonymous with *Americanization*; in the discourse of Mercosur, the world also includes European nations and sometimes is identified with novel interactions between Southern Cone countries. For a Mexican or Colombian family with various members working in the United States, globalization alludes to the narrow connections to what occurs in that part of the country where their family members live. (xxxix)

In his translator's introduction to Garcia Canclini's *Imagined Globalisation* George Yudice (2014) makes some useful distinctions among the varied 'imaginaries' that the academic discussion of globalisation has created as well. For me, this typology has been useful, as the accounts of globalisation vary significantly across their locations in academic disciplines (and, indeed across the various sub-fields in media and communications studies) and so the full range of theoretical possibilities is not always visible across the disciplinary divides. (I will admit that an earlier version of my argument in this chapter seriously oversimplified the concept of globalisation, and responses to this earlier version have helped me revise that formulation, hopefully successfully.[3])

Yudice, drawing on Martell (2007), distinguishes between three waves of theories of globalisation. The first, the globalist or neoliberal version, has globalisation as an overdetermining force that seeks free trade and economic integration under some form of global governance, and proposes the 'increasing irrelevance of the nation-state' (Yudice, 2014: xxvi, n.6). The second wave is that of the 'skeptics' for whom globalisation is 'discursive and multiply determined' and of varying political significance; for them the nation-state and regional blocs remain important, and they have political interests in reducing inequality, introducing social democracy and in managing the cultural clashes and conflicts that seem inevitable in the future. The 'transformationalists' recognise the massive changes brought about by globalisation, but resist any totalising narrative by highlighting differentiation and diversity as a counterpoint to the ideal of the global village; for these, significantly, cultural 'globalization generates hybridity' rather than homogeneity (ibid.). While this typology may not meet with everyone's assent, I have found it to be helpful in sifting through the politics and applications to which the various approaches to globalisation are inclined. In terms of which of these accounts most closely aligned with what we found in our research sites, however, the explanatory value of the more totalising accounts of globalisation was minimal. Those of the global skeptics and the transformationalists were much more useful in understanding the specific conditions that shaped the transformations in the relations between the media, the state and the community that we examined in each location.

That seems to be the message from much of the contemporary global media and communications literature, as well. In the introductory essay to their recent *Global Communication*, Wilkins, Straubhaar and Kumar (2014) acknowledge that while 'global systemic changes have reshaped the possibilities for the media in most places', 'knowing what has actually developed out of the new possibilities is considerably more complicated' (3). For them, also, the term 'globalisation' is troublesome, its application implicitly serving to overstate the extent to which the media are 'truly global in their reach and impact' when

> a large and increasing number are transnational or regional but not truly global, many remain defined primarily by national boundaries, a smaller but increasing number address cultural or linguistic regions within nations, and some are defined by the cities in which they are centred. (4–5)

And as a means of moderating some of the enthusiasm that tends to accompany each new theoretical development in media studies and which has attached itself to accounts of the globalisation of the media industries, Joseph Straubhaar reminds us of the importance of the cultural and political dimensions of the range of possibilities in play: 'most people', he says, 'experience identity with regard to media, in part, as a series of cultural geographic levels from local to global. They also experience it, depending on the place and group, as related to language, culture, ethnicity, and religion. In addition', he continues, 'identities and media use are divided still further by ethnicity and gender' (Straubhaar, 2014: 22). The economic, such a crucial driver of the neoliberal approach to globalisation, does not account for everything.

Furthermore, Garcia Canclini reminds us that globalisation is itself a phase within a much larger and longer-running, process, that of modernity (Garcia Canclini, 2014: 52). Our research also led us towards the recovery of that idea. The key factor driving the transformations we examined, the factor that most accurately caught the most widespread patterns of regional, national and local conditions in the areas under examination, was the project of modernisation. While engagement with the transnational or the 'global' was certainly widespread, the embedding of a transforming media (that is, transformations which include infrastructure, regulation and industrial development, not just the delivery of content) within a large-scale process of modernisation was virtually universal. Some locations had reached the peak of this trajectory and were merely engaged in maintaining their pace of progress, while others were just beginning. In some instances, modernisation was explicitly nominated as the objective of national cultural development policy, while in others it was seen as a means of achieving economic competitiveness within transnational markets. Importantly, cultural, political and economic modernisation emerged as the most common underlying objective for an engagement with what have been customarily described as global markets. Of course, and significantly for the focus of this chapter, modernisation is overwhelmingly, everywhere, a state enterprise.

Once you look beyond the West, it is difficult not to notice that these formations of modernity have their own histories, their own politics and their own meanings. The Western model of modernity is far from being the only game in town; rather, there are multiple, competing, alternatives, particularly in the many locations where the notion of modernity has been inescapably tainted by its historical and ideological association with the West. Marwan Kraidy explains that, for many in the 'non-West', the Western concept of 'modernity' can be regarded with considerable ambivalence. On the one hand, it 'conjures up' the potential for 'social progress, economic growth, individual emancipation, or cultural modernism', but on the other hand, it also carries the possibility for 'cultural decline, loss of authenticity and economic dependency'. In nation-states where there is a clear sense of the differences between their cultural traditions and those of the West, we can also find a 'widespread belief that modernity is incapable of shedding its Western ethos, necessitating the development of a more culturally and politically appropriate formation' that has its roots in local histories of modernity (Kraidy, 2014: 43). Deciding what might be the more appropriate formation is not necessarily a straightforward activity. Kraidy's research on reality television in the Arab states demonstrates how, as these transnational formats are taken up and adapted, the media becomes a site of contestation – not between the traditional and the modern, but rather between 'rival versions of modernity' (Kraidy, 2010: 117). This is part of an internal debate about maintaining local, national or regional control over the production of cultural identity, and about managing the uncertainties about the meaning and value of modernity while still remaining open to its prosecution. Modernity, in such a context, becomes modernities. That is, it is not a 'bounded system with a fixed, unchangeable array of basic elements', but rather a more customised vehicle, which draws upon 'different socio-economic and socio-political constellations, and different pre-modern legacies' (Mihelj, 2011: 50).

The introduction of the notion of multiple modernities should not be taken as simply relativising modernity, merely helping us to recognise the local variants of a common concept. Nor should it be seen as downplaying their power and importance – the precise content of specific formations of modernity seriously matter in their own contexts. In *Ordinary People and the Media* (Turner, 2010), I discussed the controversy that developed around the national reception of the Malaysian reality TV programme, *Akademi Fantasia*. I was reporting on a complicated debate within Malaysia about the significance of the enthusiastic response from younger audiences to this programme, which had worried certain sectors of the community because it elicited performances of personhood from its participants that were at odds with the traditional values of the society (Maliki, 2008). *Akademi Fantasia* was developed from a transnational format, and so the pleasures it offered were the product of media globalisation. However, the core factors driving the controversial reception of the programme were more to do with the strategic political and historical conversations around the contested experience of modernisation this society was facing. I still turn to this as an example of the argument I am making in this section: that in order to properly understand the story of cultural contestation within this nation over media representations of cultural and personal identities, we need detailed consideration of the specific cultural, religious and ethnic histories behind Malaysia's engagement with its national project of modernisation, which is certainly implicated within, but not reducible to, its engagement with the forces of globalisation.

As these examples hopefully demonstrate, then, once we extend our horizons beyond the standard reference points for an Anglo-American media and communications studies, the relations we may track between the nation-state and the media, as both entities engage in one way or another with the 'desire for modernity' (Ma, 2012; Pertierra and Turner, 2013), tell us quite different stories to those cited at the beginning of this chapter.

Conclusion

Let me now briefly recapitulate what I have tried to establish in this chapter. My first objective was to challenge the assumption that I take from neoliberal theories of globalisation: crudely, that globalisation is the main game, and the nation has become irrelevant. While the nation may have dropped off the radar of some of the Anglo-American versions of international media and communications studies for some time, abstracted from the dominant strains of analysis and debate, it has never been far from the centre of arguments about the media elsewhere – including in the two largest media markets in the world, India and China. In many locations today, particularly where broadcasting and print remain dominant presences, the relation between the media and the nation continues to be central to the building of the national community and constructing citizenship. It might be less central in locations where broadcasting, in particular, has declined in importance, but I would be hard-pressed to nominate a nation-state where the media did not effectively play that role to some extent, some of the time. That function continues, to varying degrees, everywhere. On the other hand, the power of globalisation, I would argue, has been subject to some exaggeration, and a degree of ahistorical oversimplification; the various 'waves' or versions of the concept indeed reflect that there is still some theoretical development to do. I am also attracted by framing globalisation in the way I cited Garcia Canclini as doing: as the latest phase in the rolling out of modernity. Since modernisation is always a national project, this approach reinforces the need to pay attention to the details of how modernity is defined and operated in individual nation-states. That process of definition, as well as the manner of its operation, directly involves the media.

Once we start to pay attention in this way, we find that there have been some significant shifts – cultural, economic and political – in the range of ways in which the media and the nation-state have collaborated in the project of modernisation. The decline of 'central televisions' (Dayan, 2009), and the manner in which the commercial media has been variously integrated into national programmes of modernisation, have been among the factors implicated in the restructuring of the power relations between the media and the state. As an example of one kind of collaboration, we find that, as the rhythms of globalisation and marketisation have built momentum, the partnership between the media and the state which generates the discursive construction of the national imaginary has begun to direct its messages towards a new addressee. Rather than addressing the national citizen, this partnership is about constructing a national identity for consumption by transnational, if not global, markets. The materials employed in this strategy tend to be familiar – the formations of national, ethnic, religious or regional identities that are already in place. But rather than being a cultural or political project, as one might once have expected, this seems to have a largely commercial objective. In certain locations now, the media has become the prime mover in the commercialisation of national identities, and the transnational marketing of these identities through nation-branding and the like. The structure of this process, in turn, impacts upon the nature of the imaginaries under construction. As Mihelj observes, 'increasingly, audiences worldwide are being addressed as imagined communities of consumers, thereby displacing alternative forms of national imagination' (Mihelj, 2011: 43). The national identity is turned into a commodity, and the beneficiary of the marketing of that commodity is as likely to be the media organisation as the state.

Consequently, as these patterns start to unfold around the world, each in their particularly located formation, I am inclined to argue that the media–state relation may now be more central than ever before. I would also argue that this is possibly because the range of ways in which it is configured, managed and directed is now more structurally and politically diverse than ever before. For those working in media, communications and cultural studies, therefore, this is not a relation that should be dismissed – neither as a 'zombie category' nor as a relation we assume we already understand. It should be interrogated closely – not only because it remains fundamental, but also because its functions have been transforming significantly under the marketising influence of the globalisation phase of modernity, and the increased commercialisation of media systems around the world.

Notes

1 This is the central argument made in Pertierra and Turner (2013: 6), through the introduction of the concept of 'zones of consumption'.
2 This was a preconference for the 2013 ICA conference in London, titled 'Global Media and National Policies: The Return of the State'. I should also acknowledge that this chapter also draws upon my contribution to a plenary panel on television and the nation at the 'Television in the 21st Century' conference at the University of Michigan in 2013. I would like to thank the organisers, Terry Flew and Amanda Lotz, respectively, for the opportunity to contribute to these really outstanding events. A version of the material presented to the ICA conference is published in the collection Flew et al. (2015) *Global Communication and National Policies: The Return of the State*.
3 I am grateful to Michael Curtin for graciously performing that task, and hope he finds less in this current version to concern him!

4
RETHINKING MEDIA REGULATION

If, as I argued in the previous chapter, the nation-state has not gone away, one of the key elements in its continuing relationship with the media remains the design, establishment and management of national regulatory regimes. The re-invention of the media has posed some difficult problems for regulators and for media policy in general. Regulation frameworks devised for an individual platform or medium, for instance, are no longer appropriate for a multi-platform environment in which content is remediated and repurposed across platforms on an industrial scale, and where previously clear distinctions between platforms have become blurred. On the other hand, the pragmatics of the policy domain might incline us towards continuing with elements of such an approach where possible. Nonetheless, some platforms are easier to regulate than others, and some platforms may be successfully managed, still, within unilateral national regulatory regimes, even though others would require transnational agreements. Notwithstanding such pragmatics, it is difficult – actually, so far, impossible – to conceive of how one might effectively deal with the *whole* of the contemporary media manifold within the one national regulatory regime. Establishing an appropriate regulatory approach to some of the core activities of the contemporary media has become extremely complicated due to (among other things) the blurring of the private/public binary in connective media, the dramatic increase in the activity of pro–am content generators online, and by the media's migration across policy jurisdictions – both intra-national and transnational – as a result of the growth in online commodity consumption. How, for instance, might a regulatory regime consistently distinguish between public and private utterances circulated via a hybridised social media? Should the amateur producers of user-generated content online be subject to the same codes of practice which apply to the production of professional content? And how do we best respond to the fact that the expansion of online media into electronic commerce takes us beyond the jurisdiction of media and communications regulation and into the world of retail and consumer protection? Most significantly for my interests in this chapter, it is probably fair to say that the transformations in how the media is produced, distributed and consumed have outstripped the capacity of regulators to devise a robust strategy for ensuring that the media, all of the media, does not behave in ways that are against the public or the national interest – while, at the same time, ensuring that media proprietors are not denied the stability of a commercially viable operating environment. And this, of course, is just at the national level.

It was much easier in simpler times. The dominant regulatory concerns during the mass media era look quite straightforward in comparison. In dealing with the broadcast media, most Western states regulated ownership and control in order to limit the concentration of media power, and to ensure a diversity of points of view; there was the national responsibility of ensuring the probity of media companies and proprietors, often through licensing arrangements or other modes of centrally authorising media ownership; and there were a range of political and national interest concerns to do with the particular structure of the industry in each state (the public/private mix, the allocation of spectrum, and so on). Early on, in many environments (most of the European states as well as in the UK, Canada and Australia) there were regulations aimed at ensuring a certain level of commercial as well as political independence – that is, limiting formal associations with business as well as with government. (The issue of the media's independence has rather dropped off the agenda for media studies as well as for governments in recent times, but Bennett and Strange [2015] do revisit and update these debates.) In the case of the print media, in addition to state regulations about cross-media ownership and a regime of ethical and legal prohibitions around defamation, slander and privacy, industry regulators typically concerned themselves with establishing codes for ethical professional practice. Finally, for all media but particularly for broadcasting, it was common for regimes of media regulation to be articulated to national cultural policy objectives (Meikle and Young, 2012: 173) – ranging from the protection of the local production of television content, as in Australia and Canada for instance, to subventions aimed at maintaining the viability of quality independent newspapers, as has occurred in France and Sweden, for example. All of this was, largely and more or less unproblematically, a matter for the individual nation-state.

As the media has mutated, however, and as the market has begun to supplant other regulatory mechanisms across national and transnational economies, there are many locations where interest in regulating the media in order to protect the public interest has waned significantly. Over the last decade or two in the UK and Australia, for instance, we have seen a considerable winding back of what had earlier been quite fundamental objectives for the regulation of the ownership and control of the media industries, for the diversity and inclusiveness of their content, for their operational and editorial commitment to public rather than merely commercial interests, and for the ethics of their professional practices. While I would not necessarily agree with a view that says the deregulatory mood we can detect in these jurisdictions constituted a trend of global proportions, there is evidence that in many Western democracies over the 2000s, state interest in or support for media regulation around these issues (that is, media ownership, diversity of media content or representation, and the ethics of professional practices) diminished. The reasons most often proffered for such a trend were either that such things were best left to the market to sort out, or that the industry environment had changed so substantially that there was no longer any need for the state to continue to play a role. In relation to broadcasting, for instance, it was commonly argued that government regulation had simply become unnecessary in the multi-channel environment. In the UK, as the centrality of broadcasting declined, as alternative choices proliferated, and as television in particular was 'transformed', the government took the view that 'legislative safeguards protecting programme quality and diversity were less called for' (Curran, 2011: 110).

Given the widespread policy preference, in the most highly modernised economies, for prioritising the individual's freedom to choose among the variety of possibilities offered by expanding free markets, it is not hard to see why selecting regulatory strategies which simply set out to maximise freedom of choice for consumers seemed a more attractive option than maintaining more strategically and politically structured public interest regulatory regimes that were increasingly difficult to design and to defend – especially to those segments of the market whose behaviour was directly affected. Not that many policy-makers have been inclined in that direction over recent years. As Des Freedman has noted, 'contemporary policymaking is far more comfortable when dealing with questions of technology and infrastructure than when it is engaging with purposeful or progressive interventions into media structures' (Freedman, 2015: 120.) Most have preferred to just leave it all to the market to sort out. Once there is a free and open market, the circular logic of the neoliberal song sheet goes, you can trust consumers to make choices in their own interests; these choices will influence the range of opportunities provided by the market, and thus the market will work in the interests of consumers. Where markets operate in that way, it is suggested, there is little need for state support of media organisations such as public broadcasters; the extensive privatisation of public broadcasters in democratic states in Europe is just one consequence of this policy orientation. Unregulated markets tend to work in the interests of capital, rather than consumers, of course, but nonetheless this version of market optimism also seems to have exerted a significant influence in the modernisation (and, often simultaneously, the marketisation) of non-democratic, even authoritarian states, as noted in the previous chapter, where the liberalising of regulatory control over some areas of media content and over the structure of the media industries can also be seen. In general, then, this was a period in which we can discern a clear tendency, among governments of many different political hues, to shift the responsibility for overseeing the media's service to the public interest from the state to the market (Meikle and Young, 2012: 181). This 'paradigm shift in media regulation', reflected a fundamental change in the understanding of the role of, most particularly, broadcasting in society 'away from the notion of a public good to a notion of information as a commodity' (Voltmer, 2013: 148).

It is possible we are reaching the limits of this phase, now. As the commercialisation of the media is becoming a more noticeable feature of the media landscape, it has generated some pushback. There is a revival of political interest in moderating the influence of the market on the function of the media for the consumer and for the citizen. Concern about the decline of publicly funded broadcasting, the commercial challenges to the continuing viability of an independent quality news media, especially in print, and the effects of market forces on the diversity of media content, are all live issues in various locations around the world at the moment. Furthermore, there are particular concerns which have also engendered closer consideration of how the community might responsibly manage what happens online: a key concern here is consumers' surprising acquiescence in the compromising of individual privacy that has become commonplace in so many commercial transactions online. As we saw earlier in this book, even though many consumers appear to be prepared to sacrifice their rights to privacy under certain circumstances, there are plenty of critics, and indeed some legislators, who recognise the dangers of allowing this to go unregulated; children's online exposure, for instance, to commercial exploitation, to bullying and to pornography, have all been proposed as limit cases of media use that should be properly addressed within a civil society.

In what is perhaps an even more significant shift, there are also questions about some quite central assumptions upon which media policy in the West, in particular, has long been founded: that is, the imputed relationship between a liberal media policy regime, a free and (most often, commercial) independent media, and the development of a democratic polity. Some outside the West, for instance, have begun to argue that the principles underlying the regulatory regimes within the democratic states in the West, while unexceptionable in themselves, have not necessarily translated easily, or beneficially, into other political and cultural contexts. While we may once have assumed these principles were, in a sense, universally applicable, Katrin Voltmer (2013) has recently argued, in a book that I will draw upon later in this chapter, that they are in fact proving to be far more context-dependent than their proponents had originally realised. The implications of that argument are far-reaching, with the potential to dramatically change how we think about the politics of media regulation in the present conjuncture and into the future.

The range of issues I could take up in relation to this topic is extraordinarily broad as well as often specific to the locations and to the regulatory regimes in question. I cannot hope to provide here a comprehensive overview of the problems and opportunities for media regulation in the present; that would be a book in its own right. My objective in this chapter is much more modest, and its mode is more illustrative than cartographic. I don't have my own answers to the problem of how we regulate the media properly today; but I do believe that regulation remains necessary as long as we continue to think it is important that the media should operate as a core component of the public sphere in a democratic polity. That highlights what is really the first task for us: as citizens, reclaiming the political will to nominate this as an issue we need to take seriously and, as media studies academics, reviving our appreciation of the centrality of such considerations to our professional interest, and acting upon that appreciation. My own objective here is to make the case for that revival of political will. In this chapter, the examples of shifts in the structure and function of the media I discuss, each in their own way, direct us back to the central issue of how contemporary regulatory strategies might ensure that the re-invented media operates not only in their own, but also in our, interests. Rather than focusing on issues around a regulatory regime which is primarily concerned with the maintenance or structuring of viable commercial environments for media proprietors, therefore, I have chosen to deal with some examples of concerns that go to the regulatory objective of protecting the public interest or advancing the public good.

Privacy, journalism and the public interest

If we are now to revisit the media's relation to the public interest and/or contribution to the public good, it is not before time. Policy debates about the media over much of the last two decades have been dominated by a very different set of questions: typically, how regulation might be minimised in order to optimise the unrestricted operation of the market (as has largely been the case in the US) or conversely, in some cases, how it might actually protect and maintain the oligopolies the market has already produced (that's the story in Australia). Both of these strategies (amazingly, and despite their contradictoriness!), have been represented by their advocates as pro-competition, pro-market and pro-business. Notwithstanding that little conundrum, in general it is the case that explicitly pro-market measures have become so thoroughly established within media policy that they have generated concern outside the industry about the extent to which their effective privileging of market leaders works against the interests of the citizen and the ordinary consumer. (Of course, it is precisely such a concern that motivates the early enthusiasm for the promise of interactive digital media – responding to their potential to trouble existing configurations of media power.) In this section of the chapter, I want to highlight two such areas of concern: the manner in which commercial digital media platforms have reshaped the contexts within which personal privacy can be protected; and how societies should respond to the fact that the redefinition of journalism we discussed in Chapter 2 has impacted negatively upon its continuing contribution to the public good.

Although the internet was originally developed and funded by state institutions, its recent history has been overwhelmingly one of privatisation and commercialisation. The 'additional layers' of what Andrejevic (2007) calls 'the digital enclosure'[1] – mobile telephones, mobile e-mail, texting, Wi-Fi and so on – have not only replayed this history, but they have also served to extend the purchase of the digital well beyond the traditional boundaries of media activities. In addition to the traditional spheres of media production, distribution and consumption, the digital domain has developed new marketing and monetising strategies which take us quite a way from the libertarian and democratising promise of the early internet. As digital media platforms have expanded their influence into so many of the practices of our everyday lives, there have been heightened expressions of public concern about our loss of control over our personal data, the reduced protection for personal privacy online, and the complex of issues that have emerged in response to the evolving practices of online providers – from social media sites to online retailers – which fail to provide even the most minimal level of transparency about the industry's monitoring, surveillance and data-mining of consumer behaviour (Sunstein, 2009; Turow, 2011; Andrejevic, 2013; van Dijk, 2013).

Notwithstanding the slowly rising tide of such concerns, there remains considerable debate about whether regulation or indeed the state in general does have a legitimate role to play in shaping or moderating the outcomes of the digital revolution as it unfolds:

> As virtual spaces have come commercialized and commodified, the need for policy intervention *within* the Internet is hotly debated. Some argue that the marketplace is the best regulatory tool and that if, for example, privacy issues emerge on a social network, then users will simply move elsewhere. In a similar vein, others argue that such space should be self-policed, and even though the architecture of a social network might be shaped by technology providers, individuals can determine their own privacy settings, and debate standards within their own communities, pushing back or shifting providers should the services they require fail to live up to expectations. The counter-view to this suggests that the dominance of particular actors, of the scale of the leading Web 2.0 firms, for instance, requires regulatory intervention. (Meikle and Young, 2012: 176)

As this summary demonstrates, the market optimism that overstated the political potential of the new media industries by confusing consumer participation with consumer power is also implicated in the failure of governments, and indeed, to some extent of media studies, to recognise the need for societies to address the disproportionate concentration and exercise of power.

I want to focus first on the complex of problems which have accompanied the gradual demise of personal privacy online. As I noted earlier, while many consumers may be reconciled to sacrificing some of their rights to privacy in return for the convenience of commercial transactions online (shopping, booking travel and so on), there are still significant reasons why such a sacrifice should not be regarded either as acceptable or necessary. Terry Flew has outlined three key reasons for concern about what has happened to personal privacy as a result of the development of networked ICTs and electronic commerce enabled by the spread of digital media. The first is related to the 'capacity to connect diverse information sources through networked computer bases'. This capacity means that forms of information – significantly, about us – that were once separate or isolated can now be aggregated. The resultant individual 'profiles' are the property of the organisation that collected the data; in most cases the individuals concerned are unaware of their profiles' existence, and they operate in ways that meet commercial objectives which may or may not have any concern for the specific individual involved. The problem, especially but not only within a democratic polity, is that this information may be acquired for use by 'commercial or government agencies in ways that are not appropriate or relevant to the organisation acquiring the data or the purpose [for which]... the information is used' (Flew, 2007: 153). Flew's second issue is less sinister, but still, one would think, an area for some regulation and control: that is, the manner in which online transactions are used to develop an 'electronic trail' of individuals' consumption and information-gathering patterns, which is then used to push unwanted information to those individuals through spam, junk mail, targeted advertisements on social media and search engines, and so on (Flew, 2007: 154).

Finally, Flew points to what seems to me a most fundamental issue, which is the fact that consumers seem to have accepted somehow – slowly, implicitly, but also in a sense unwittingly – that online activities can be assessed against a different ethical standard than similar activities undertaken offline (ibid.). Not only do we seem to have agreed to relinquish the rights and safeguards that are already in place to protect us offline, but we have done so without establishing an alternative and equivalent regime of protection in the online world. Of course, the borderless character of the digital space has played a significant part in limiting the point of any such regime; after all, how effective would a unilateral national regime turn out to be in most circumstances? As a result, there is still little in place that mandates an appropriate level of transparency about the commercial collection and use of information about individual consumers. On the other hand, the combination of the technological affordances available, and the commercial advantages to be had from making use of them, means that there are now substantial commercial incentives for, and thus an enhanced likelihood of, 'government and corporate surveillance over individuals through utilising the capacities of ICTs and electronic networks' (ibid.).

The incremental manner in which the digital enclosure has extended its purchase, and the ideological legacy of the internet's libertarian and individualist origins, may have delayed the recognition that some of the behaviours it supported may have regressive political consequences. The strength of our desire for the capacities that digital media provided, as we searched for information online and shopped for commodities across the globe, may also have encouraged a view that this domain deserved to be allowed some special tolerance, exempting it from the consumer protection regimes that applied in the offline economy. It was, after all, a key component of the realm of 'cool capitalism' (McGuigan, 2009). Furthermore, the interactivity on offer (and the hyperbole used to promote it) may also have encouraged users to believe they were in control themselves, and therefore not at the mercy of commercial providers who might turn out to be unscrupulous. Whatever the reasons, many consumers have proven to be strangely unconcerned about the possible risks as they respond to 'the invitation to participate in their own manipulation' by providing 'increasingly detailed information about personal preferences, activities and background' to those who will 'use this knowledge to manage consumption' (Andrejevic, 2007: 242). And, of course, the gradual commodification of our data happened out of sight, and without our consent. The data-mining industry developed initially as a by-product of the new affordances of interactivity, and has only subsequently evolved into becoming a major component of the online business model.

The interesting thing about this dimension of the re-invented media is how far it travels beyond something we might once have unequivocally labelled 'media'. Much of what I am describing involves e-commerce, but it is thoroughly enabled by and articulated to the key media components of the digital enclosure – social media, interactive media, user-generated content, mobile telephony, search and online video-on-demand – which have become so thoroughly embedded within the marketing processes of the retail and services industries, that it can be hard to determine what is 'media' and what is not. (As clear a demonstration, one would think, of the processes of mediatisation as one could find.) As a result, the regulatory problems canvassed above are partly to do with the sheer difficulty of disentangling the multiple skeins of variously mediated activity implicated in the operation of online commercial enterprises. Even the most fundamental questions remain unanswered: what activity do you actually regulate, and through what kind of regime? Any regime designed specifically for regulating transnational online activity would require multilateral arrangements between nations – and ideally, all relevant nations.[2] It is even more difficult to imagine how we might do this in a way that might protect the public interest, as it is variously conceived, in each of these participating nations as well. It is this last consideration – the question of how the re-invented media might continue to serve the public interest – which takes me on to the second area I want to consider.

We have heard a great deal about the so-called 'crisis in journalism' (for example, in Curran, 2011; McChesney, 2007; Dahlgren, 2009; Meikle and Young, 2012). This is not only a commercial crisis about the viability of traditional versions of journalism and in particular about the future of the newspaper, but it is also and more importantly a crisis of authority and integrity which in some locations is leading to calls for the reform of the current frameworks for the regulation of the practices of the news media. Among the most dramatic provocations for reform has been the *News of the World* phone-hacking scandal in the UK, but they would also include the manner in which television news outlets such as Fox News have developed a brand which has effectively eliminated the distinction between reporting and opinion (I do realise, of course, that talk radio in the US and in many other locations eliminated that distinction from their formats decades ago!). More broadly, it is clear that the expanded provision of news and information we discussed in Chapter 2 has not achieved the projected outcome of expanding the range of sources and voices which go into making up our news diet. Rather, the same market forces which produced a highly concentrated, oligopolistic and commercialised traditional media sector, that prioritises entertainment over information, have generated similar outcomes online. In such an environment, the future of a journalism dedicated to serving the public interest, and thus constituting a public good, looks to be under threat.

Of course, there are some within the convergence culture camp who welcome this as an inevitable and democratising development, usefully undermining the established patterns of media power. The hyperbole with which this possibility is typically addressed, however, does little to substantiate that position. This, from Mark Deuze:

> Journalism, as it is, is coming to an end. The boundaries between journalism and other forms of public communication – ranging from public relations or advertorials to weblogs and podcasts – are vanishing, the internet makes all other types of news media rather obsolete (especially for young adults and teenagers), commercialization and cross-media mergers have gradually eroded the distinct professional identities of newsrooms and their publications (whether in print or broadcast), and by insisting on its traditional orientation on the nation, journalists are losing touch with a society that is global as well as local, yet anything but national. (Deuze, 2007: 140)

Deuze provides no evidence for this extraordinary series of claims, and the assertion that society is now 'anything but national', in particular, is impossible to take seriously.

This remains a minority position, however, and while there are certainly complicating arguments coming from those who are concerned with introducing greater historical depth to the contemporary accounts in order to retrieve continuities that have been overlooked (Zelizer, 2015), the crisis in journalism has become a relatively standard topic for inclusion in synoptic accounts of the current condition of the contemporary media. Robert McChesney's account is typical in its focus on the unravelling of professional standards and the falling investment in quality journalism, nominating the 'decline of investigative reporting, the degeneration of political reporting and international journalism, and the collapse of local journalism' as core symptoms of a situation that is 'acknowledged by all but the owners of large media firms and their hired guns' (McChesney, 2007: 94). These trends have been in place for some time and they are responsible, most agree, for the apparent decline in the community's trust in the authority and legitimacy of the news. Public opinion polling, in many locations around the globe, reflects the low esteem in which the profession of journalism is commonly held. In the US, Andrejevic reports, 'despite (or perhaps because of) the proliferation of hours devoted to television news, not one major news outlet was trusted by the majority of the American people' (Andrejevic, 2013: 3). Instead, 'poll after poll have revealed declining levels of trust in news outlets and a heightened sense of perceived bias on the part of journalists' (ibid.).

An additional, and crucial, factor here is the heightened commodification of news and the view from commentators, as well as from those who are the objects of journalists' inquiry, that the news media are no longer primarily concerned with serving the public interest, and therefore that the service they offer can no longer be regarded, unequivocally, as a public good. In her critique of the UK news media's treatment of the disappearance of the toddler Madeleine McCann, Mirca Madaniou argues that the 'private lives and tragic circumstances' of Madeleine's parents were 'effectively sold for advertising revenue' (Madaniou, 2013: 186–187). She quotes from Gerry McCann's witness statement to the Leveson inquiry, where he expressed the view that the editors of a number of the newspapers chasing the McCanns' story, such as the *Daily Express*, 'considered their ability to make money from the additional sales of the newspapers carrying the stories to be more important than taking into account our legitimate concerns as to the accuracy of the reporting and the effect it would have on our family' (187). Far from denying this accusation, Madaniou says, it was not even 'contested by the editors themselves'. To the contrary, the editor of *The Sun*, Trevor Kavanagh, stated in his evidence that 'news is as saleable a commodity as any other; newspapers are commercial, competitive businesses, not a public service' (ibid.). Citing Natalie Fenton's (2013b) comment that 'in certain quarters the notion of press freedom is synonymous with the freedom of the market to do as it pleases', Madaniou concludes by making the point that 'collapsing freedom of expression, democracy and the free market in one category is not only conceptually flawed but also practically dangerous' (ibid.). Since the newspapers' treatment of the McCanns inflamed public opinion against them, resulting in death threats, personal abuse and perhaps even some disruption of the police investigation, that does not seem an exaggeration.

These are not just issues of taste, then – of an elite squeamishness about tabloid journalism or the vulgarity of celebrity content. This is about the fundamental social and political function of the news and, ultimately, about the abuse of media power. The crisis of journalism is to do with the widening gap between the news media's conventional claims to operate in the interests of the public and as a central component of the furniture of a democratic state on the one hand, and the cynical, unethical and harmful practices that have evolved in recent years in response to heightened levels of commercial competition within the industry, on the other. In such a commercial context, it seems, those newspapers which hold to the more ethical and disinterested practices of a more traditional version of the fourth estate are less able to compete for today's readers, and thus face the risk of extinction. Angela Phillips has argued that this is a situation which should be addressed by state regulation:

> [I]f society believes that news media has a dual role, and should also support and facilitate democratic debate, then it has to provide the same safeguards as it does to ensure that the education system functions for the good of society and not merely for profit. News-gathering and dissemination is not a profit-making business unless it is combined with entertainment and celebrity news, and heavily supported by advertising. In order to underpin the democratic functions of news and free it from over-reliance on gossip and scandal, in a fiercely competitive online environment, news organizations may also need a degree of subsidy. (Phillips, 2013: 267)

Phillips describes the measures taken in certain Scandinavian countries to ensure a higher level of 'professionalism' in their newspapers through government subsidy:

> Research by a number of scholars has demonstrated that 'publicly subsidized newspapers in Sweden and Norway tend to provide more original, in-depth, and multiperspectival coverage than their advertising-dependent counterparts' (Benson and Powers, 2010). In both the Netherlands and Norway (Humphreys,

> 1996) government subsidy is tied to editorial freedom. In Norway there is recognition (by the courts) that journalists require editorial freedom from the pressures of the markets as well as the pressures of the state. (264)

A similar programme of subsidies occurs in Denmark, aimed at ensuring diversity and 'a reasonable balance of political views in the national press' (264). In examples of other, smaller-scale, regulatory initiatives aimed at better protecting the public interest elsewhere, ordinary people in Brazil enjoy a legally binding right of reply to media reports, enabling them to correct misrepresentations and giving them at least 'a small fraction of the power that news organisations assume for themselves' (267).

If we wish to see the news media continue to play the dual role that Phillips describes, one that most still claim to regard as vital to a free society, we need to ask if it is acceptable for media proprietors to be accountable only to their shareholders. There is a wider issue of accountability for most media institutions here that, in my view, the steady progress of marketisation has pushed aside, resulting in the tendencies that are now widespread across Western democracies. As Couldry, Madaniou and Pinchevski (2013: 6) point out in their introduction to *Ethics of Media*, the 'issue of the accountability of media institutions was at the heart of the phone-hacking scandal and its aftermath' (the Leveson inquiry), but this is far from the only context where issues of the media's accountability to its public arise. Furthermore, it is clear that the kind of accountability Phillips suggests should be required by the community is not something that the contemporary news proprietor would readily accept. Commercial imperatives have come to dominate the media's practices and, increasingly, their view of themselves, and so it is little wonder that, as Couldry *et al.* acknowledge, 'discussion about how to build new institutions for regulating the media has only just begun' (ibid.).

It is a discussion that should proceed, however, even if in many ways it is wearily reminiscent of the early debates around the development and structure of the broadcasting industries in most places when they were established. The debates then were about the competing entitlements of the proprietor or media institution, the nation and the public; while commercial viability was a factor at that time, it was not nearly as powerful a factor as it has become subsequently. In general, as the political reliance on the market as a means of distributing opportunity has become more entrenched, the commitment to protecting the public interest has declined. We are now facing the consequences of this. In both examples surveyed in this section of the chapter – the threat to personal privacy posed by commercial practices online, and the threat to the survival of independent news journalism from increased commercial competition – the market has produced outcomes that may be commercially satisfactory. However, they do not serve the public interest at all well and may even reduce the social benefit of the media to the point where they may no longer be considered a public good. Standing against these trends, in most cases, are regulatory systems which are inappropriate or no longer fit for purpose in the changed circumstances of the re-invented media. There is an urgent need to rethink, and to debate, what is required for these changed circumstances.

The media and democracy

If the changing platforms, structure and function of the media present their own challenges for regulatory policy, this is not the only difficulty faced by the nation-state attempting to develop a viable framework for media policy. As nation-states have emerged from authoritarian or socialist rule in Central Europe, Africa and Asia, and as they begin the transition towards democracy, they have tended to regard the creation of a liberal and independent media as one of the preconditions for this transition to succeed. In order to do this, in the first instance at least, they have typically drawn upon the established Western models of a democratic media, and adopted their approaches to media regulation. In their application, however, these models have often been modified or tailored to the local circumstances – drawing criticism as these transformations are seen by outsiders as constituting a worrying dilution of the principles they embody. There is now, however, a different kind of criticism which questions what had hitherto been taken for granted – the relevance and appropriateness of these models as they are taken up, in particular, by non-Western societies. Katrin Voltmer's (2013) impressive comparative study of the media in 'transitional democracies' argues that the adoption of regulatory regimes based upon Western democratic models does not necessarily have their desired effect – that is, her evidence suggests, they will not necessarily assist in the transition to democracy nor in the development of an independent media.

As we noted earlier, Western liberal models of the media have traditionally regarded them as one of the cornerstones of the democratic state. On the one hand, the media play a role in creating the fully informed citizen required for a properly functioning democracy and, on the other hand, the 'fourth estate' role of the media protects the interests of the citizenry by holding government to account – publishing comment and criticism, checking the accuracy of government information, and uncovering information in the public interest, while observing protocols of ethical practice in order to guarantee the legitimacy of their own activities. That the media should operate in this way is more or less taken for granted in Western democracies, but this taken-for-granted-ness is built upon the implicit normatisation of their experiences (Hallin and Mancini, 2004). Once we move beyond that context, and most media theory and research published in English still does not do that very often, we encounter many more variations in the structure of the political relations between the media and the state. The media are not necessarily or inherently democratic; indeed, they 'serve dictatorships as happily' as democracies. What makes the media a democratic force are 'the particular norms' of the institutional structure within which they operate and 'the quality of their performance' within that context (Voltmer, 2013: 23). These factors vary across regions and between nations even within the West. While Norway, Denmark and Ireland, for instance, are all subject to EU regulations and are all part of that one market, 'their communications policies remain distinct, and are linked to different welfare systems and different political cultures' (Mihelj, 2011: 37).

There has been, however, a degree of political naivety among both scholars and policy-makers about just what might be achieved via a liberal media. It is an attitude that Mihelj criticises, saying that 'media and communication scholars have time and again fallen prey to technological determinism, abstracting the media from the context in which they operated and treating them as an autonomous modernizing force' (59). The most recent example of this attitude, as we have noted earlier, can be found in the projections of political change connected to the rise of new media, but it has a much longer history. It has long been implicated in Western interventions into national development projects elsewhere (particularly in the global South), in which the mass media were expected to 'lay the groundwork needed for successful modernization': to 'inculcate modern work routines and health habits, instil cultural attitudes favourable to innovation, cooperation and long-term effort for the common good, and lure the population away from traditional customs, fatalisms and superstitions' that might 'stand in the way of progress' (ibid.).

Voltmer's research tells us that this is much easier said than done – notwithstanding the West's considerable political and historical investment in exporting a package that assumed an homology between the ideals of Western democracy and liberal models of the media. When these models are put into practice within environments that have very different cultures and circumstances to those of the West they can have unexpected and negative consequences:

> [T]he experiences of the last two decades or so, when radical neoliberal economic reforms, premature elections and uncurbed media liberalization have frequently resulted in more inequality, violent intergroup conflicts and political polarization, ... [suggest the need] for a greater sensibility for the specific conditions under which transitions are taking place outside the Western world. (Voltmer, 2013: 5)

The conditions to which Voltmer refers are those that have framed the experience of many transitional democracies – mostly states emerging from authoritarian regimes, such as the nation-states created out of the former Yugoslavia, for instance – and they are conditions where a thorough commitment to the principles of media freedom can prove difficult to maintain, at least in the short term:

> Many new democracies are deeply divided societies emerging from bitter ethnic, religious or ideological conflicts, and the danger of the return of the monsters of the past remains present for a while. In these transitions, democracy-building and nation-building take place at the same time, creating a highly complex and fragile situation. More often than not, the measures that are necessary to cope with each of these parallel processes are difficult, sometimes impossible to reconcile. Several countries that have emerged from civil war have taken measures to restrict public speech that could contribute to intercommunity hostilities. (Voltmer, 2013: 40)

Consequently, Voltmer argues that even though the Western model of democracy and the liberal model of an independent media remain, for 'many journalists, policymakers and citizens alike', desirable ideals, neither of them can be 'easily exported to other parts of the world'. Indeed, 'the more that non-Western countries are adopting democratic forms of governance, the larger the divergence between the "original product" and its local implementation becomes' (5). There are many reasons for this. Some we have met in earlier chapters, such as 'the growing scepticism among democracy activists in non-Western countries about the desirability of becoming like the West' (ibid.), as well as resistance to what can be represented as a process of cultural and political colonisation. Another factor is the nature of the Western values embedded in these ideals; in Asia, in particular, the West's valorisation of the individual is often inconsistent with longstanding cultural traditions and social values. Almost inevitably, Western models of a liberal-democratic media run up against local insistence on the importance of self-determination – and not just in terms of maintaining political sovereignty but also in terms of ensuring the political, cultural and media structures that are developed have their roots in local values and traditions:

> As societies struggle to free themselves from Western dominance, they also aim to find their own way into a democratic future. In a complex process of 'domestication', the norms and practices of democracy and democratic journalism are reinterpreted in the light of local cultures and experiences and adjusted to the needs and constraints of everyday life, which often differs dramatically from the relatively secure and wealthy circumstances in advanced Western democracies. (ibid.)

Of course, insistence on a sensitivity to local values and traditions, and the tailoring of media systems to align with them, can also be motivated by less respectable political objectives; it can be used to legitimate the persistence of authoritarian practices and to mask a reluctance to recognise the rights and obligations usually supported by democratic systems. While Voltmer clearly acknowledges such a risk, she nonetheless argues that if we are to set up regulatory structures which will work in these transitional democracies, 'the norms of democracy and free media have to be contextualised in the light of the specific historical, cultural and political circumstances in which a particular new democracy emerges' (11).

There is also the related issue of the models of journalism that are appropriate to different contexts. Voltmer encourages her readers to reconsider the case for 'development journalism' (sometimes called advocacy journalism), a model that has been criticised for its surrendering of journalists' autonomy to the requirements of a central policy agenda. Voltmer admits that national development goals can still be used to 'muzzle' journalists and 'delegitimise critique', but on the other hand it 'puts the interests of the people first', and has the potential of constructing a professional role for journalists that, at its best, 'incorporates democratic principles of checks and balances as well as the responsiveness to the social problems that trouble their countries' (202).

The provocation to Voltmer's research – the perception that a one-size-fits-all regulatory approach to the development of a democratic media does not necessarily produce positive results – was also reflected in the positions taken by a number of the participants from outside Western Europe who attended the ICA preconference on regulation and the state I referred to in the previous chapter. In particular, these participants were insistent that, in their own experience, there was often no option but to significantly modify the models they had adopted. They were concerned that this should not be misread, from the outside, as constituting a reduced commitment to the development of democracy in their country. Rather, they argued, there was a significant social and political benefit to establishing some limits on what was said through the media when their paramount concern was maintaining the stability of what had been hard-won, but fragile, national political settlements. It is a position that is familiar within debates about media behaviour in Asia as well (Sun, 2009). Voltmer is unflinching in confronting this ethical challenge and arguing for some flexibility here:

> National media are frequently used as a means to limit pluralism and to promote a unifying national narrative. Not surprisingly, this instrumentalization of the media regularly triggers criticism from international media development groups. But in societies that are at risk of disintegration or even sectarian violence, a stricter control on who is saying what in the public sphere might be the lesser evil. (Voltmer, 2013: 19)

It is probably important to point out that the market will not help here, despite the fact that among the favoured means through which a liberal view of the media seeks to moderate such control, and to ensure the media's independence from the state, are privatisation and commercialisation. The curious ideological elision between marketisation and democratisation we discussed in the previous chapter plays its part here, with consumer choice mistaken for political power. However, in most places there is little to prevent political forces, both state and non-state, from controlling or indeed owning commercial media. Such arrangements are common in Latin America, for instance. Voltmer (2013: 9) warns that 'privatization and commercialization are not a guarantee for media independence as liberal theory would suggest', and Madaniou's comment, cited earlier, is worth reiterating: that 'collapsing freedom of expression, democracy and the free market in one category' is 'conceptually flawed' (Madaniou, 2013: 187). Indeed, the market has the capacity to act as a spoiler in the democratic public sphere, with commercial media prepared to act directly against the public interest if it suits. In Chapter 2, we noted instances in the Balkans where commercial media cynically exploited ethno-nationalist tensions in order to generate an audience. That seems to exemplify the situation that Fenton (2013b) describes – where media freedom can mean, in effect, that the media can do anything it pleases, whether it is socially damaging or not. Fenton's comments, of course, were provoked by the situation in the UK and that raises the possibility that even in established democracies there may be legitimate reasons to consider more restrictive regulation, on the media's intrusion on private individuals for instance, in order to prioritise a particular conception of the public interest over the democratic principle of an entirely open media, on the one hand, and the untrammelled operation of the market, on the other. While always likely to be a controversial suggestion, the homology so spuriously, but nevertheless successfully, constructed between democracy and the market has made even the discussion of such a possibility more difficult than it might once have been.

Conclusion

The changes that have occurred over the last two decades – as media platforms emerge, as media use hybridises, as technological convergence mutates into new patterns of media concentration, and as audiences fragment – have often been cited in support of the proposition that the scale and diversity of the contemporary media market makes concerns about the public interest redundant. In my opinion, there is plenty to suggest that this is not so. What I have been canvassing in this chapter, may well seem an old-fashioned set of debates; they are, in a sense, because they have been with us more or less since the beginning, and for good reason. Notwithstanding the scale and complexity of the media's re-invention, the key questions about what society needs from its media have remained more or less unchanged since the establishment of the broadcasting industries: their answers must involve the establishment of an appropriate settlement between the interests of the state, the public and the market within the context of a modern democracy. The precise terms of these settlements will vary, depending on the political and social makeup of that context, but they will not be adequate if they do not contain some checks and balances upon the influence of the market. An effective regulatory system must ensure the media's professional and economic viability, of course, but it is also the case that 'without effective action and the willingness of the government in power to act in the wider public interest', the media tends, over time, to 'fall into the hands of whoever has the means to hijack them to their own interests' (Voltmer, 2013: 135). Journalism is in danger of losing crucial elements of its unique democratic role as it confronts the new realities of the expanding media market for information and entertainment, and the commodification of information threatens to turn social media and search engines into mere feeder sites for e-commerce. The arguments laid out in this chapter are meant to give some urgency to the need to rethink the role that regulation should now play, in this reconfigured mediascape, as a means of retrieving those aspects of the media's social function that are now at risk, and that we do not want to lose.

While this process of 'rethinking' media regulation has taken me back into some familiar territory, I am not arguing, in the end, that nothing has changed. A great deal has changed, but that should not divert us from focusing on what, nonetheless, remain fundamentally important factors in our understanding and experience of the media – in the present as much as in previous eras. Even though the focus in recent years has been on the changing modes of consumption and the continual evolution of media platforms and applications, it is important we do not lose sight of the need to properly understand the structural conditions within which these changes occur, and of the need to properly examine the social, political and cultural implications of these changes in all their diversity. If we want the re-invented media to serve our interests in ways that go beyond merely providing us with new opportunities for consumption and entertainment (and why shouldn't we want that?), and if we are prepared to seriously consider how that might occur, then we must begin to review the possibilities for regulatory interventions which might protect the public interest against those vested political and commercial interests which would compete with it. As I say, such an enterprise now is more difficult than it has ever been before, but that only makes its prosecution more critically important.

Notes

1. This is defined as 'the creation of an interactive realm wherein every action and transaction generates information about itself'. 'The Internet', Andrejevic (2007: 2) argues, 'provides the paradigmatic example of a virtual digital enclosure – one in which every virtual "move" has the potential to leave a digital trace or record of itself.' The choice of the term 'is meant to invoke the land enclosure movement associated with the transition from feudalism to capitalism, the process whereby over time communal land was subjected to private control, allowing private landowners to set the conditions for its use' (3).
2. The digital optimists were correct when they argued that regulating what happens online is not easy for individual nation-states to do unilaterally, due to the borderless character of so many of the transactions which occur online. Where they were wrong was in arguing that it was impossible. It can indeed be done, but the qualification here is that those states which have been most effective in their management and control of digital and connective media are also those with the least commitment to democratic principles, and thus also the least threatened by political or ethical criticism of the interventions required.

PART III
The consequences of celebrity

5

THE CELEBRIFICATION OF THE MEDIA

The pervasiveness of celebrity is widely recognised – how could it not be? We have watched celebrity content migrate from the 'redtop' tabloids and supermarket newspapers into the colour supplements and 'front pages' of the websites for newspapers with much higher, 'quality', aspirations. We have seen celebrity gossip spread from its early base in mass market women's magazines onto blogs and websites such as *TMZ*, eventually becoming 'news' as it takes its place in the full range of news and magazine formats – from *National Enquirer* to *Time* magazine, from breakfast television chat segments to prime-time network news bulletins, from shock jock radio interviews to conversations with experts on public talk radio. While the consumption of celebrity has long been a relatively discrete component of everyday life for citizens of highly mediatised societies, the current era is one in which the boundary between the world of celebrity and that of the everyday seems more porous than ever before. 'Ordinary people' now have new opportunities to achieve the public visibility and attention associated with celebrity (Bonner, 2003; Turner, 2010). The most prominent of these opportunities, of course, is through participation in reality TV formats such as *Big Brother, The Bachelor, Jersey Shore* and so on, as well as docu-soaps such as *Airport* or *Driving School*, and lifestyle or makeover formats such as *What Not to Wear*. In addition, there are the growing number of 'YouTube celebrities', ordinary people who have attracted a following through their presence on YouTube, and in some cases have earned millions of dollars from the income generated by pre-roll advertisements (the top earner for 2014 was PewDiePie, estimated at US$7 million) (Warner, 2014). Less noticeable, perhaps, is the extent to which social media has adopted the discourses and values of celebrity as the default setting for a hybridised process of self-fashioning (hybridised, that is, as a networked media process with both private and public dimensions). Alice Marwick's *Status Update* argues that the subjects of her research, young professionals working in the technology industries in California, live in 'a society where status is predicated on the cultural logic of celebrity, according to which the highest value is given to mediation, visibility and attention' (Marwick, 2013: 14). The link between the construction of a public persona and the establishment of social status, Marwick suggests, has become fundamental for many young professionals in the US as they 'adopt self-consciously constructed personas and market themselves, like brands or celebrities, to an audience or fan base' (5). They do this by using social media tools learnt from Twitter, Facebook and YouTube, as well as the 'marketing and advertising techniques drawn from commercials and celebrity culture' (10). We will return to Marwick's analysis of this phenomenon in Chapter 6.

Of course, these days, celebrity culture has permeated other spheres of activity as well. Some time ago, Corner and Pels described how 'celebrity power' had been progressively 'translated from the popular entertainment industries towards more "serious" fields such as business, politics, art and science' (Corner and Pels, 2003: 8). Modern 'mediated politics', they argued, has 'foregrounded issues of "style, appearance, and personality", breaking down some of the fences that separate politics from entertainment and political leadership from media celebrity' (2). Indeed, politics has learnt from the production of celebrity and appropriated its strategies for the development of a public persona; as Kristina Riegert notes, the 'systems and techniques used to produce media celebrities differ little from those used to promote political personae' (Riegert, 2009: 6). As a result, Corner and Pels (2003) suggested, politics has become something of a 'culture industry', 'increasingly resembling a talent show or popularity contest, where polling is as relentlessly continuous as in the music and film charts, and star-gazing and infotainment have become equally central as they are to the tabloids and the celebrity magazines' (8). It's not only politics, however: witness the rise of the celebrity CEO in the world of business, and their personal identification with the branding of their enterprises and their visibility in the public sphere (Littler, 2007; Boyle and Kelly, 2010). Even in what is still the comparatively rarefied world of the contemporary university, as it transitions from thinking like an institution to behaving like a corporation, there is evidence of the take-up of the strategies of celebrity: in the university where I work, senior administrators have earnestly urged us to make better use of our 'research rock-stars' in our marketing strategies! In general, whatever field of endeavour it is that seeks public visibility, it is now almost routinely the case that it would make use of the tools, the discourses, and perhaps some of the values, of celebrity to achieve it. Little wonder, then, that some in media, cultural and communications studies have argued that we are experiencing the 'celebrification of society and culture' (Driessens, 2013), or that we have already become a 'celebrity society' (van Krieken, 2012).

The focus of this chapter is just slightly more restricted than that. We will talk more about the discourses and values of celebrity when we consider the social function of celebrity culture in Chapter 6, but my intention in this chapter is to argue the proposition that we are experiencing something which may well amount to the celebrification of the media. In support of that argument, I will outline one key example of this process as an illustration of the role that celebrity culture has played in the re-invention of the media. Typically, and so far, most discussion of celebrity's pervasiveness has focused on the power, ubiquity and (often) the superficiality of celebrity content rather than examining the character and scale of the industrial changes that have occurred in connection with the expansion of the production of celebrity content for the mainstream media – and the effects of these changes on the structure and practices of the media industries in general. Of course, any such examination would find that celebrity has not produced these changes on its own. In most of the instances one might nominate, it has acted in concert with, for instance and at least, the logics of commercialisation, the associated rise in the privileging of entertainment content over information, and the increasing concentration of media ownership around the globe. Although I certainly wish to argue that celebrity is a major factor in its own right, it is important not to lose sight of how it is implicated in the broader patterns of change we have been tracing throughout this book. Notwithstanding the many press reports dealing with what they customarily represent as a deplorable increase in our interest in celebrity culture, there are some suggestions that it is not necessarily the focus of the audience's interest that has changed. James Curran has pointed out that stories about ordinary people and celebrities were the 'most-read' categories of content in daily newspapers way back in 1963; what has changed in the contemporary context, he argues, is not so much audience preferences for celebrity stories, but rather the extent to which media outlets have progressively skewed their contents towards satisfying such preferences as a priority (Curran, 2011: 165). It is this shift in media practice – a major component of the re-invention of the media – that is the most significant consideration here. In this chapter,[1] I take up that issue by looking at just one area of media production – news – in order to outline some of the ways in which celebrity is contributing to changes in how the news is gathered and delivered by the media, as well as in what now counts as the news.

Producing 'celebrity news'

It would be fair to say that the rising tide of celebrity news has not so far been accompanied by a correspondingly rising tide of respect for this domain of journalism. The term 'celebrity news' itself is something of a provocation; it would be easy to regard it as a cynical appropriation of the discourses of legitimacy that authorise 'genuine' news and so it is not surprising that the term should be met with some scepticism. Indeed, I can recall that the first time I heard the label 'celebrity news' – in association with the TV programme *Entertainment Tonight* – it seemed risible (just as when I first saw the descriptor 'a news entertainment' on the masthead of the British tabloid, *Sunday Sport*, in the late 1990s). The phrase seemed hopelessly oxymoronic; indeed, the very fact that such a combination of terms could be proposed seemed destined to devalue the currency of more conventionally 'serious' versions of journalism. Over time, however, and as the connection between news and entertainment strengthened across platforms and modes of distribution, and in the generation of content, the 'celebrity news' formulation has lost much of that early sense of dissonance. Today we have mass market magazines that present themselves unproblematically as 'news' magazines even when all they deal with is celebrity, with perhaps some 'human interest' stories thrown in (the examples I have in mind include the top-selling US magazine *People*). In general, 'celebrity news' has settled down now into being a widely used industry descriptor for the reporting and commentary on celebrity. The fact that it is widely used, however, does not alter the fact that it remains a compromised term; for many, celebrity news is still not an entirely respectable branch of journalism. (It should be noted that this is not necessarily a bad, nor even an unwelcome, situation for those producing it and selling it.) Nonetheless, the gradual normalisation of the term effectively masks the fact that many of the practices used to produce celebrity news are significantly different to those used to produce what is more conventionally described as news. What I would like to do first in this discussion, then, is to highlight some significant specificities which distinguish the industrial production of news about celebrities from the practices of more traditional forms of journalism.

Perhaps the most significant factor which distinguishes 'celebrity news' from 'the news' is that, more than just about any other domain of news (with the possible exception of business news), news about celebrities is overwhelmingly managed by those who are generating it – that is, by the celebrities themselves, through their personal or organisational promotions and publicity machines.[2] If the standard[3] version of the production of news has the news journalist independently developing sources in order to seek out information that would otherwise be hidden and which the public needs to know, then celebrity news is probably the direct opposite to this. For a start, news about celebrities is usually generated by those closest to them, and mostly for commercial rather than informational purposes. It is generated via direct contacts with the news organisations; it is most often intended to serve the interests of those at the centre of the story by giving that story as wide a distribution as possible; and in terms of its contribution to public interest, it is probably only the public's level of information about the range of available entertainment choices that is likely to suffer if they don't have access to the story in question.

Notwithstanding, celebrity has now become a fundamental component of the news across all media platforms. As journalism has become more commercially competitive, as the news cycles have dramatically shortened, and as the populations of newsrooms have declined, the news is increasingly the product of information provided directly, and mostly unsolicited, to journalists. However, even within that general industrial context, the extent to which this is true of celebrity news is exceptional. Unsolicited celebrity news is provided directly to journalists via press releases, press packs, access to events, through personal contact with the publicity and promotions organisations generating interest in new commercial vehicles (films and television productions, for instance), through the publicity arm of the celebrity's own management team, and often through offers of access to the celebrities themselves. The supply of this material, and these approaches, far exceeds the demand; as the size of the publicity and promotions industry has grown, the contemporary journalist is drowning in press releases, event invitations, promotions material and so on. This means that the publicist has to work exceptionally hard on the presentation of their promotional material in order to lift their product out from the pack, while the journalist merely has to select which stories they most want to run with. The promotions industry caters to the journalist's needs by doing as much as they can to make their story 'ready to run'; when that is done properly, the journalist is required to do very little to make use of it. Strategies include providing tailored video, high-resolution sample images and so on, as well as taking care that the press release is written in a news-compatible form. In a time-poor and highly competitive profession, there is little the journalist can do (indeed, wishes to do) to defend themselves against such strategies. Consequently, rather than acting as an old fashioned news-gatherer, the celebrity news journalist becomes a filtering agent, sorting out their choices from the plethora on offer but doing little by way of independent investigation, fact-checking or backgrounding. In this way, the practices upon which celebrity news is built are very different from the practices upon which traditional modes of news journalism were built.

Nowhere is this more evident than in the journalist's participation in the media event – the event designed by the 'smiling professions' (Hartley, 1992) purely in order to generate media attention (Boorstin, 1971). The journalist is invited along to these events – not so much to ask questions, but really just to be a witness. If the journalist turns up, if their attention is rewarded, and if they decide to record that publicly in some way, then the media event becomes news and free publicity results. The journalist, of course, is perfectly aware that they are being used as an instrument for turning advertising into news; they cooperate, however, because they need to ensure they continue to be kept in the loop by the major promotion companies, and accorded the level of access they need to cover their beat properly. The interdependence thus generated – that is, the journalist's dependence upon their sources within the entertainment industries and the entertainment industries' dependence on the journalist to publicise their products – creates a level of cooperation between the journalist and their sources that is equivalent, ultimately, to what might once have been described as being 'captured' by their sources (Davis, 2003: 35). While, again, it is worth noting that this is far from being the only domain of news that is subject to this (business journalism and political commentary are the other main contenders here), it may well be the one where the practices such capture would necessarily entail have become the most routinised and industrially embedded.

Underpinning all of this is the close relation between the gradual evolution of these practices of newsgathering and the massive expansion in the public relations, publicity and promotions sector in most modernised economies since the 1980s.[4] As Davis, notes, the co-existence of journalism and public relations, while never part of the 'fourth estate ideal', was not a serious matter while 'public relations remained an undeveloped and under-resourced profession', and while journalists retained a certain level of 'day-to-day editorial autonomy'. However, he concludes, that is no longer the case 'for either industry' (Davis, 2003: 31). The growth of the public relations industry in recent years has 'assumed exponential proportions' as it has developed into a major industry (Cottle, 2003: 3). In the UK, which is the object of Davis' analysis, the number of public relations firms increased from a total of 46 in 1967 to 2,230 in 1994 (Franklin, Hogan, Langley, Mosdell and Pile, 2009: 8); Frances Bonner, David Marshall and I found an equivalent increase when we examined the growth of public relations in Australia over roughly the same period (Turner, Bonner and Marshall, 2000). Globally, and despite the occasional interruption from economic downturns such as the global financial crisis, the public relations and publicity industry has continued to record double digit annual percentage growth rates into the present (Sudhaman, 2014). While the relation between the expansion of this service sector and the rise of celebrity culture, including celebrity news, is complex, and while the specific histories of its development vary significantly across different locations (in Australia, for instance, its emergence was initially closely connected to the government-funded revival of the local film industry), there is a symbiotic relationship between these two developments. In his account of the power of celebrity in contemporary culture, Chris Rojek argues that there is a direct connection between the rise of celebrity and the emerging 'power bloc' that he calls the 'public relations–Media hub': the 'gatekeepers between corporations, celebrities and the public' (Rojek, 2012: 22). In *Understanding Celebrity* (Turner, 2014b), I also emphasise the importance of the public relations and promotions sector's gradual integration into the industrial structure of the media: this, I argue, affects not only the production of celebrity but also the production of a mediated public culture in general – something both John Hartley, in his analysis of 'the smiling professions' (Hartley, 1992), and Andrew Wernick in his influential diagnosis of 'promotional culture' (Wernick, 1991), had picked up well before the celebrity industry had got thoroughly into its stride.

In the late 1990s, Frances Bonner, David Marshall and I undertook a research project which examined the production of celebrity in Australia (Turner *et al.*, 2000) through, among other things, investigating the importance of the role played by the public relations and publicity industries. What we found was virtually a collaborative relationship between public relations and publicity professionals, and those producing the news. (That characterisation of the relationship was, I should acknowledge, often disavowed by those professionals we interviewed; as Davis notes, the 'influence of public relations practitioners … [has] always [been] much greater than scholars recorded, journalists admitted, or news consumers were aware of' [Davis, 2003: 31]). This relationship was by no means confined to the production of celebrity news but rather extended into the production of news more generally. For instance, we found the proportion of business news that was based on corporate public relations' press releases which ran largely in their original form, was as high as 80 per cent even in the high-end 'quality' press. Other studies found similar patterns elsewhere; Bob Franklin made equivalent claims for the UK (Franklin, 1997), while Rein, Kotler and Stoller (1997) claimed that '70% of all information that is published as news' in the US 'originates in publicity and public relations' (Turner, 2014b: 50). Subsequently, academic interest within journalism studies has focused much more intently on the relationship between journalism and public relations as a significant and widespread structural shift in the production of news over the last thirty years (Cottle, 2003).

All of that said, if the collaboration between public relations and publicity practitioners and journalists has become an institutionalised component of the news industry in general (which is what I would argue it has become), this is especially, indeed exorbitantly, the case with the production of celebrity news. The power and purchase of the public relations and publicity sector constitute the basic industrial conditions for the rise of celebrity news. It is hard to imagine another production model which could generate the volume of material now produced by the publicity and promotions industries for circulation through the news media. The scale of the output, the avidity with which it is taken up, and the degree to which it has become industrially embedded in the production practices of the news media across all platforms, entitle us to think of this as a significant restructuring of the industrial production of news journalism. In the next section, I want to consider what I would also regard as a further distinctive aspect of the production of celebrity news: its degree of dependence on the availability of the image.

The rise of the image

This may not, at first glance, seem like an especially crucial or distinctive feature of the production of celebrity news; most categories of news, but particularly television news, are driven by the availability of the image. However, I think there is a case for arguing that celebrity news is driven by the availability of images more routinely than any other genre of news; rather than the image being used as an illustration of, or the authority for, the news story, much of the time the celebrity image *is* the news story. Some have argued that mass media celebrity has its historical origins in the moment when newspapers began to publish images of individuals in the late nineteenth century, and it is commonplace to talk about this as the moment when the public shifted its interest onto the image of the newsmaker, thereby personalising and thus complicating our assessments of his or her achievements (and implicating us in what Hartley [1992] has called 'the politics of pictures'). While this has been true for quite some time, among the key factors involved in the heightened availability of celebrity images in recent years has been the expansion of the activities of the paparazzi, the (in some ways related) development of the complex array of fan sites, celebrity news sites and official celebrity sites accessible online, and the increasing use of social media by celebrities and their followers.

To take the paparazzi first, the development of print media interest in celebrity images that took off in the mid-1980s, coupled in the West with the relaxation of the standards affecting what people might expect of such images – the increasing number of 'candid', naked or otherwise unauthorised shots – expanded the market for the paparazzi shot of the famous person. Mortensen and Jerslev claim that paparazzi photography 'presently constitutes the largest genre of visual celebrity news on the internet', along with 'red carpet photography' – that is, the staged and structured photo opportunities provided for the mass media in general (Mortensen and Jerslev, 2014: 620). However, the prominence of the paparazzi photo is not confined to the internet. Whereas, earlier on, paparazzi photography occupied a 'marginal, though conspicuous, position in tabloids and gossip magazines', it is now at the 'centre of mainstream news and entertainment culture, and is distributed broadly across media platforms, including gossip and entertainment sites, mainstream news media, fashion magazines [and] ... social media' (ibid.). Consequently, there are more outlets, more competition, but also a more globalised market for the high-profile photo; the financial rewards for selling an image have grown substantially as it is sold on or syndicated around what has become a highly concentrated corporate media environment. Kim McNamara has published a very useful discussion of the role of the paparazzi in the production of celebrity. Responding initially to a context in which there had been a significant decline in the print media's employment of staff photographers and an increasing use of freelancers, McNamara notices a 'profound shift in the nature of the paparazzi industry' in recent years. Whereas once it was largely composed of freelance photographers, 'selling directly to picture editors at news and entertainment publications', now, she says, the field is 'dominated by multinational agencies with their own brand of mostly web-based entertainment news' (McNamara, 2011: 516).

It is commonplace, of course, to regard the paparazzi as a parasitic formation rather than as a structural component of the industries which produce celebrity. 'Paparazzi are fairly despised and are fairly despicable', says Fred Inglis, but he points out nonetheless that 'we feed eagerly on the photos':

> When the wolves took off in pursuit of Princess Diana and her driver, slightly drunk, took up the challenge, raced away in the huge black Mercedes, and crashed into the underpass concrete to kill himself, her, and her temporary suitor, the Arab princeling and playboy Dodi Fayed, the gross and deadly photographs fetched a fortune. Not many people looked away. (Inglis, 2010: 265)

Despite the initial disgust at the circumstances of Diana's death, the tactics used to secure such photographs have not reduced the appeal of the paparazzi's product. The textual characteristics of a telephoto shot of a famous person living their normal life unaware of being observed (slightly blurry, often with a series of shots presented to compensate for the fact that no one photo on their own has enough interest), have become signifiers of a kind of grubby authenticity – I would suggest because of, rather than in spite of, their clear demonstration that someone's privacy has been invaded. Indeed, Mortensen and Jerslev (2014) argue that the authenticity thus constructed is articulated to a discourse which is about penetrating to the 'ordinariness' of the celebrity's life; as they put it, the mundane character of the context for such photos takes 'the extra out of the extraordinary'.

As these images have transitioned from being staples of low-prestige or tabloid publications and become instead quite routine elements of mainstream news production, paparazzi photography has gone from 'being a street-based job to a technology-driven industry' (McNamara, 2011: 517) with an increasing orientation towards the mass distribution platforms such as *Mail Online*. McNamara points to several factors which have contributed to the growing impact of the paparazzi on the mainstream and traditional media. Paparazzi images have played a decisive role in some of the major circulation battles across the print media, and their importance in the strategies of competition is reflected in the extraordinary prices paid for highly sought-after images (such as candid photos of Angelina Jolie and Brad Pitt). The commercial importance of the paparazzi influence also seems to lie in the role they have played in what has become quite fierce competition across the convergent mediasphere. The fundamental strength of the market demand for images of celebrity across formats and news genres means that they are highly valued by virtually every medium and distribution platform:

> The traditional model of paparazzi exploitation of website images of a star is based around a steady stream of low-charge, high-volume sales, with occasional exclusive shots. At a time when advertising spending in traditional media is declining, paparazzi websites are thus trying to boost advertising sales in new media outlets ... The economy surrounding a star like Britney Spears encompasses multiple industries such as magazines, newspapers, TV and the web, but feeds ultimately from the paparazzi industry whose pictures are bought to help a story sell. (McNamara, 2011: 518–519)

Paparazzi agencies have become a new kind of news provider, responding to the development of new media sectors by 'offering a specialist service in breaking celebrity news' (523). Their exploitation of the online environment, McNamara argues, has only enhanced their importance:

> The Internet has broadened and 'elasticized' access to, and flows of, celebrity images ... Paparazzi agencies bring audiences the images of celebrities, but it is the increasingly sophisticated technology – mobile phones, MP3 players, BlackBerrys – which allow the viewer to access images and information in new ways. Thus, the significance of paparazzi agency entertainment websites lies not only in the simultaneity of their production of fan-oriented content, and outsourcing to other news and entertainment agencies, but also in the web's speed and ability to reach a mass audience. (522)

The decision of the paparazzi agencies to go online and develop their own web presence has contributed greatly to the number of images in ready circulation, as Marshall (2006) says. However, the second factor in this – and still a relatively new one in the history of celebrity – is the decision of many celebrities to cut out the middle man entirely and represent (or perhaps more accurately to perform) themselves directly to their audiences through celebrity websites and blogs, social media and more recently through mobile photo-sharing applications such as Instagram. 'Official' celebrity websites can involve anything from the posting of the standard press releases and publicity shots to more frank and perhaps even genuine discussions of the celebrity's own thoughts and personal life. High-profile celebrities who have been known to use these sites to communicate directly with their fans in this way include Beyoncé, Ashton Kutcher and Mariah Carey. Such use of these sites has the capacity to significantly change the character of the relationship between the fan and the celebrity; indeed, Marshall suggests that in some areas (popular music and sport are the ones he nominates) it is becoming an expected element, indeed a transformation, of the fan–celebrity parasocial relationship (Marshall, 2006: 640). Certainly, it is becoming an increasingly common strategy for the individual celebrity to employ as a means of bypassing both the promotions industry (ironically, those employed to develop and manage their *own* public persona) and the news media – at least in the first instance, since whatever is said or displayed on these sites is thus fair game for the evening news (and sometimes becomes a serious problem to be addressed by the publicist whose expertise has been sidelined). The specific value of Instagram to celebrities is relevant here, because it enables them to regain some control of the supply of images to the market.[5] They are able to choose what is circulated, and that is desirable, but there is also the added consideration that the greater the currency of their Instagram feed, and the more they get picked up by the mainstream media, the less the demand for unauthorised images from the paparazzi. Furthermore, images are circulated free on Instagram, whereas paparazzi photos are sold. Already there is anecdotal evidence that some paparazzi are finding that Instagram is affecting their business.

Then, there are, of course, the amateurs – the bloggers, the passer-by with the mobile phone, or what have been called the 'citizen paparazzi' (the label appropriating, of course, the implications of a pro-social politics associated with 'citizen journalism'). Not only has the ordinary person taken to populating the web with images located on their personal blogs or on fan-sites, but amateur photographers have managed to get their material into the commercial mass media as well. While there are still some industrial firewalls limiting access to some of the print media, those media platforms which depend more vitally on immediacy have been keen to take up images produced by amateurs with their mobile phones. The low-resolution aesthetic of the professional paparazzi photograph I referred to earlier actually assists these citizen photographers because it blurs the distinction between what a professional image and what an amateur image looks like, and thus removes one of the barriers to participation in a market that is consequently more open now than ever before. The use of citizen paparazzi or ordinary people to provide both images and story content is now common in celebrity websites such as *TMZ* and in its TV version. Ordinary people can also act as scouts (or, less respectfully, celebrity stalkers), alerting *TMZ*, for instance, to the location of likely targets (such as, notoriously, Britney Spears), so that the *TMZ* stringers with their digital cameras can head for the scene. Further assisting the most committed celebrity stalkers is the existence of commercial services that can help you track the current location of your chosen celebrity!

Finally, on this issue of the expansion of the trade in and the availability of the image, there are, of course, hundreds of thousands of both commercial and DIY websites and blogs devoted to celebrities and while many of them will contain comments and chat, a great many of them are simply offering pictures: screen shots from movies, publicity stills, 'candid' shots and so on. There are also websites which specialise in what one calls 'celebrity skin' – naked or near naked shots of female celebrities. While we might not have much respect for these, they help to make up the gene pool for some of what eventually makes it onto more respectable news sites. Some of these naked shots will eventually migrate into mainstream journalism, appropriately pixilated or otherwise modified, if they can be connected to a story. This genre existed well before the internet, of course (*Playboy* built a mini-industry on it, while at the lower end of the market the magazine called *Celebrity Skin* had been around for years), but the internet has increased the ease with which this material could be accessed and the opportunities for doing so in relative privacy, as well as providing the capacities for copying, sharing and networking. The result is a dramatic expansion in the supply and accessibility of images of celebrities over the last decade or so.

Gossip as news

A further factor which distinguishes celebrity news from more traditional news, it has to be said, is its attenuated relationship with the facts. Simply, celebrity news does not need to be 'true' to be interesting; its status, as Dayan (2009) has said of much of what happens via social media, is closest to that of rumour – and for most of its audience that is enough. Nevertheless, for the rumour to be worth circulating widely, there has to be some confidence in the source. Celebrity news reporters have to find ways to establish their credibility by demonstrating the quality of their access to the sources of celebrity news, rather than by proving their capacity to deliver verifiable, evidence-based stories. Two of the generic features of the production of celebrity news emerge from this. As is also the case in some other genres of news – politics, or sport, for instance – successful celebrity journalists build their reputation as expert commentators, drawing on inside knowledge that is, almost by definition, unverifiable. Just as prime-time television news bulletins will have their report from the day's doings in Parliament or Capitol Hill, in which a specialist political correspondent will provide informed comment and analysis, so too, breakfast or morning magazine programmes will have their specialist celebrity gossip reporter in LA or London, previewing the latest productions from the entertainment industry while also relaying the latest gossip and rumour about high-profile celebrities. As is also the case with so much of the coverage of politics, a great deal of this reporting is openly speculative and effectively free of any requirement to provide supporting evidence[6] – indeed it is the acknowledged freedom from the rules of evidence that makes the speculation both possible and interesting. The second feature is that, unlike reporters bound by more traditional notions of journalistic objectivity and independence, the presentation of celebrity journalism will readily foreground (or actively construct) the friendly personal relation between the journalist and their subject; it is almost required that the performance of the successful celebrity journalist directly invokes an off-screen familiarity with the celebrity being interviewed. This not only provides a frame for the interaction between the two, but it seems to have become necessary as a means of authorising the celebrity commentator's observations and speculations. This subverts the standard ethical model of the relationship conventionally constructed between the journalist, their sources, and the subjects of their enquiries.

The gradual establishment of such a discursive regime around the presentation of celebrity news reflects the media's more general and progressive, if implicit, tolerance for the redefinition of what it might regard as news. Celebrity is not the only area where this is notable (again, in sport, politics and, less obviously, business news there is also quite a bit of tolerance for this), but celebrity is probably the key area where we can see consumers most readily accepting gossip or rumour as news.[7] Of course, to some extent this has always been the case – the role of gossip in what used to be called the social pages, and the role of the gossip columnist, have a long history (see, for instance, Gabler, 1995). I would argue that in this earlier context, however, the role was quarantined rather than pervasive: that is, gossip was confined to the relevant column or section of the paper, rather than being the front page story (as it can be quite often now). Nonetheless, not to give too categoric an assessment of changes that demand a greater degree of nuance than I can give them here, it is certainly true that the celebrity commentator of today and the gossip columnist in that earlier formation do share a number of attributes. For instance, it is their acknowledged distance from the facticity of news that actually makes what they do possible: no-one is going to call them to account for making a wrong call because 'getting it right' is not the point in this domain of news. It is the performance of the speculation, which invites a response – of engagement and further speculation – from the audience, that is the point. Producing celebrity gossip as news is, then, a cooperative cultural production, a pleasurable collaborative narrative in which, ideally, the audience is as much implicated as the journalist.

In themselves, some might argue, the practices I am describing here do not reflect a broader paradigm shift for the profession of journalism since, as I say, they could well be regarded as simply the most recent version of the longstanding tactics of the gossip columnist. That is not my view, however. To indicate why I am not convinced of this, let me refer to a video that appeared on the website of Australia's only national daily newspaper, the NewsCorp-owned *The Australian*, some months ago. As part of a discussion of the Australian universities' contribution to journalism training (something on which the paper had been commenting for some time in order to challenge the notion that a university degree would necessarily contribute positively to the profession!), the editor of *The Australian*'s Higher Education Supplement, Julie Hare, was joined by the editor of the Media section of the paper. Since there had been much discussion in the newspaper about what was needed to train a good journalist, Hare asked her colleague to tell her what he would regard as the fundamental motivation for his own personal engagement in journalism. His response: 'Well, we all love gossip, don't we?'. Hare seemed a little taken aback by such a cheerfully superficial response – defining news as gossip – but did not challenge it.

The exchange certainly demonstrated why *The Australian* might believe that a university education is unnecessary for training journalists today, but it was unusual, and revealing to have the newspaper present such a crass construction of the news on their own official site. Today's news organisations tend not to be quite that candid. Rather, from time to time, even the most commercial media proprietors find it is in their interest to reassert their commitment to the traditional definitions of the news – to the ideals of serving the public good and informing the processes of democracy. Typically, such claims are trotted out when individual news organisations are faced with significant political, legal or regulatory challenges; in the UK, the Leveson inquiry into phone-hacking is only the most recent provocation for this kind of thing. So, while there are occasions when it is in the commercial interest of the proprietors of news organisations to publicly distance themselves from the kind of shift I am describing, and from comments such as that quoted above, in order to reaffirm their commitment to the traditional role of the fourth estate, there is also reason to regard such reaffirmations with scepticism. If the evidence given to the Leveson inquiry is any indication, the notion of the fourth estate in such situations, it seems, can operate as a convenient ideological refuge, a strategy of last resort, for news organisations that seem actually to 'have lost interest in journalism', and the 'incentive to produce it' (McChesney, 2007: 214). As the media move more towards the role of providing entertainment rather than information (Turner, 2010) – which is what the tabloid newspapers, Fox News and *Entertainment Tonight* all do – and as serious attention to the more old-fashioned news formats such as political current affairs declines, then celebrity news may indeed turn out to have played a significant role in displacing the population's interest in other forms of news (Couldry, Livingstone and Markham, 2007).

Conclusion

The lower cultural status accorded to celebrity news has to do with its compromised relation to more independent and traditional versions of news, and its implication in some of the changes that are occurring in how the news is understood as a cultural and informational form. Celebrity news is both a product, and an appropriation, of news journalism which largely provides entertainment for its consumers while serving the commercial, and at times organisational, interests of those with an industrial stake in publicising (the) celebrity. It has adopted a number of the practices and discourses of news while also establishing some practices and discourses of its own, and it has successfully colonised parts (sometimes, all!) of many of the sites and platforms once occupied by other versions of the news. While celebrity news satisfies many of the same cultural demands as news – with gossip an overlapping factor – I am suggesting that it also serves some very different functions to those traditionally attributed to journalism. In addition, it has its own particular system of industrial production which is tightly articulated to the needs of the entertainment industries, and their publicity and promotional arms. Not to be too precious about it, of course, traditional journalism is itself far from pure in this regard; there are many periods in its history when it has addressed the entertainment needs of the population as a major consideration. Celebrity journalism is far from the first to treat the news as a means of entertaining its audience. It may, however, be the first genre of news to see that as, in effect, its primary (perhaps its only) objective.

This is an account of celebrity's implication in the re-invention of only one area of the media, but it is a crucial area, and there are more. There would be little point in my denying the fact that my personal assessment of the ascendancy of celebrity content and the concomitant decline in other categories of news is, on balance, critical; while I am unconcerned by the popular pleasures and meanings that celebrity news generates for its audiences, I am concerned by its ongoing displacement of more conventional formations of the news – the scale of celebrity's dominance has had the effect of shrinking the news. That said, the point of the approach taken in this chapter is not to mount that critique. Rather, the chapter sets out to outline an illustrative example of how the industrial mutations that have contributed to the establishment of the routinised production of celebrity have changed significant elements of the industrial structure used to produce the news. The proposition that celebrity has played a major role within the re-invention of the media does not only depend on the observation that it is now an ubiquitous genre of content; rather, and more importantly, it depends upon the demonstration that the rise of celebrity has changed what the media does, and how it goes about doing it. The celebrification of the media, then, is structural as well as discursive, and that has significant implications for the media's social function. It is to that issue – the social function of a mediatised celebrity culture – we will turn in the following chapter.

Notes

1 An earlier version of the material that follows was published as Turner (2014a); I am grateful to the editors of *Journalism* for the permission to draw on this material for this chapter.
2 There are many accounts of how this works, including Turner, 2014b.
3 I accept that there is now such variation across platforms and such volatility in the news industries overall, that it is becoming very difficult to invoke a 'standard' mode of news production; hence my recourse to the notion of a 'traditional' set of news production practices as a means of signifying a regime of practice that is still conceptually, ethically, ideologically and practically dominant, and therefore still recognisable, but which may not maintain that practical dominance for much longer in the face of other models of production.
4 In the US, this process began earlier, in the 1950s, although it accelerated dramatically again in Reagan's America in the 1980s.
5 It should be acknowledged, however, that there are certainly plenty of press reports which have revealed the existence of a degree of professional collusion between members of the paparazzi and the celebrities they follow. An arrangement that benefits both parties, this results in what look like candid, everyday life, snaps of the celebrity in question, and thus have the authenticity and revelatory implications carried by the more intrusive paparazzi shots, but the photo opportunity and perhaps even the selection of the pictures to be circulated has been arranged in advance.
6 However, at least commentators on politics acknowledge the need to refer to their sources – even if they are unable to name them, there is the expectation that they do actually exist. Celebrity journalists can get away with backing up their stories by referring

in vague terms to some zeitgeistian 'buzz' they have picked up from 'what people are saying'.
7 However, I am not suggesting that this means this material is given the same factual status as other kinds of news. As Gamson (1994) has shown, consumers of celebrity news can be extremely savvy about just how much to believe; for many of his informants, it is clear that the entertainment value of celebrity news may well have little to do with whether or not audiences believe it to be true.

6

INTERVENING IN THE SOCIAL

The function of celebrity culture

If it is possible to demonstrate that celebrity has changed what the media does, it is much less easy to demonstrate that celebrity has changed what we do with the media. Yet the ubiquity of celebrity inevitably raises that question. Furthermore, there is constant media interest in the controversial aspects of the behaviour of celebrities – both on and off screen – which provoke debate about what kind of influence these figures have on the rest of society. Chris Rojek uses a quote from the founder of public relations, Edward Bernays, as an epigraph to *Fame Attack*, which asks:

> Who are the men [sic], who, without our realizing it, give us ideas, tell us whom to admire and whom to despise, what to believe about … how our houses should be designed, what furniture we should put into them, what menus we should serve at our table, what kinds of shirts we must wear, what sports we should indulge in, what plays we should see, what charities we should support, what pictures we should admire, what slang we should affect, what jokes we should laugh at? (cited in Rojek, 2012: vi)[1]

Bernays' answer to this rhetorical question would have been, I imagine, public relations practitioners, but today it could just as easily be celebrities. If that is so, then, there are more questions to be asked about the social and cultural consequences of a celebrity culture that is not only dominant within the mass media, but which is also emerging as a significant influence on what happens online and through social media.

During what we might think of now as the mass media era, there was plenty of discussion about the possible social effects of an emerging celebrity culture, particularly from the 1980s onwards when it started to become more prominent. Initially, it was relatively common for the cultural function of celebrities to be publicly described in quite simple terms: as 'role models' for their followers,[2] or as objects of fantasy and desire. The academic approach to these issues which took us beyond such formulations began, effectively, with Dyer's (1979) *Stars* which examined the complex historical and social relations between the particular kind of individuality the star signified and that which was valued (or, alternatively, problematised) by the society. Dyer's work generated a burst of interest in the social and cultural function of the representations of film stars. Over the 1990s, however, there was a shift in focus as media and cultural studies researchers gradually transferred their interest from 'stars' to 'celebrity' in response to the expansion in the market for celebrity content, the availability of celebrities to supply it, and the growing recognition of celebrity's cultural pervasiveness. As celebrity culture has continued to grow in both scale and influence, and as the opportunities for celebrification have multiplied and extended their reach into the everyday lives of ordinary citizens (Bonner, 2003), the category of celebrity has assumed a closer, and indeed quite different, relation to the social than that associated with 'the star'. According to Julie Wilson, 'audiences identified with stars: they looked up to them, structured fantasies out of them, and modelled behaviours after them':

> Star images were prominent cultural sites for reflecting upon the tensions and constraints of identity, as well as for reproducing dominant ideologies of individualism. Today, the salience of stardom and celebrity culture no longer emanates primarily from specific star images, the broader set of meanings they enable, and their cultural power to shape ideas about identity. Rather, the current significance of stardom and celebrity culture rests on the fact that celebrity itself is an increasingly crucial linchpin of contemporary identity in a social world where the boundaries between our public and private selves constantly shift and blur. Like celebrities, we inhabit and navigate presentational media regimes, displaying our selves to be interpreted by others. (Wilson, 2014: 434)

Celebrity culture, Wilson suggests here, has become a major component of the media's participation in the construction and performance of personal identities. Marshall (1997), Rojek (2001, 2012) and a number of others have made similar claims and the possibility that they are correct has resulted in a steady increase in the interest – from within and outside the academy – in investigating the social or cultural functions celebrities might fulfil for their audiences. Within celebrity studies, it has become more or less an orthodoxy that celebrities, in general, do indeed perform such functions, although anything more detailed or categoric than that is the focus of continuing debates. In fact, dealing with this issue is, one way or another, precisely the central problem for celebrity studies and for many working on these topics from within media and cultural studies as well. Tania Lewis (2014) and Chris Rojek (2012) have talked of celebrities as 'life coaches', providing 'free advice about grooming, impression management, self-promotion, and even "correct" social, political, cultural and environmental values' (Rojek, 2012: 139); others have argued that audiences attempt to make sense of their social experience 'through celebrating and actively identifying with the lifestyles of public personalities' (Corner and Pels, 2003: 8), or that they follow celebrities in order to perform what Jim McGuigan has called 'the popular deliberation on the conduct of life' (McGuigan, 2000: 111). While there is general agreement that celebrity contributes to the construction of cultural identities, there is no such agreement on exactly how this occurs, or to what effect.

Over time, the incremental advance of celebrity's influence – that is, not only within the media, but within society at large – has gradually injected some urgency into the consideration of such questions. Within cultural studies, characteristically, there has been an effort to understand how the popular consumption of celebrity might work as a politically progressive process. Among the favoured topics for those in cultural studies working on celebrity in the early 1990s were the gendered and at times transgressive identities embodied in Madonna's public persona (Schwichtenberg, 1992); since then there has been a continuing interest in teasing out the politics of representation for a string of individual celebrities. Over the early 2000s, digital and social media's facilitation of the DIY construction of a public persona was hailed as personally empowering; the fascination with Jennicam and the phenomenon of the cam-girls (Senft, 2008) was related to the possibility that celebrity was becoming democratised. Within the wider discussion of celebrity, however, it was, and is, common for celebrities and their fans to be regarded more censoriously. Indeed, researchers from within social psychology have pathologised the excessive consumption of celebrity as 'celebrity worship syndrome', treating it as if it was a psychological disorder (McCutcheon, Maltby, Houran and Ashe, 2004). While the discovery of this 'syndrome' was eagerly taken up within media reports, it has little to tell us about the most common modes of engagement with celebrity: it focuses upon the most extreme formations of such engagement and underestimates the complexity, and the ambiguities, of the attractions of celebrity. Gamson's (1994) early study (one of relatively few that has dealt directly with celebrity fans rather than with representations of celebrity), makes it very clear that there are a wide range of audience positions from which the consumption of celebrity may be pleasurable or entertaining. Celebrities are just as likely to attract attention for their bizarre or unacceptable behaviour (Michael Jackson dangling his baby son from a hotel window or Jade Goody racially abusing Shilpa Shetty), as for their positive achievements. Celebrity is about visibility and attention; both of these may be generated by all kinds of utterances, appearances and behaviours, producing a wide range of responses (from admiration at one end of the spectrum to ridicule at the other) from celebrity fans or from the public at large. Only some (perhaps, in the end, very few) of these responses are likely to involve anything like the helpless adulation assumed to be at the root of so-called 'celebrity worship'.

We do know something about how and why ordinary people participate in activities that promise them access to celebrity (Andrejevic, 2004; Sender, 2012), and we do know quite a lot about the nature of the pleasures that celebrity offers to those who consume celebrity content through the media (Holmes and Redmond, 2006). At this point we don't know just how, or indeed if, celebrity culture might be imbricated into those practices of everyday life that are *not* directly concerned with consuming or producing or participating in the media – in a sense, the crucial test for the extent of celebrity's cultural influence and its relation to the social that we might use to evaluate claims that we have become a 'celebrity society' (van Krieken, 2012). As I argued in the previous chapter, celebrity's pervasiveness is now a significant attribute of the re-invented media, but we still need to better understand how it might intervene in and thus affect the social life of the individual citizen or consumer. In order to do that, it is helpful to focus most closely on those areas of our mediated culture where celebrity has become, as it were, 'ordinary'.

The ordinary celebrity

Contemporary accounts of celebrity's socio-cultural influence need to accommodate the fact that the character of the discursive construction of celebrity has changed in recent years, and in ways that impact significantly on the question of celebrity's relation to the social. Initially, representations of mass mediated celebrities routinely, perhaps constitutively, explored their dual status as both extraordinary – talented, beautiful or just plain lucky, but certainly belonging to an elite – and ordinary – often revealing aspects of their personal lives which humanised them, asserting that despite the privileges of fame, deep down they were 'just like us'. Media mythologies about how a new talent is 'discovered' have exploited that duality for many years – particularly in the film and the music industries. Today, the balance between the ordinary and the extraordinary in the discursive construction of celebrity has changed, primarily, I would argue, as a result of the proliferation, demoticisation, and the consequent redefinition of celebrity that is associated with the re-invention of the media. The 'demotic turn' (Turner, 2010) in the access to celebrity is also closely associated with a shift in the industrial production of celebrity which sees some formats and platforms treating the creation of celebrity as if it were an end in itself. We have Senft's (2008) 'micro-celebrity', for instance – ordinary people using their micro-blogs and mobile social media platforms such as Twitter to develop a networked fan base that can, in certain cases, translate into a more mainstream mass media profile. Television, in particular, no longer only exploits the celebrity created via another platform; it also creates its own celebrities from whole cloth through reality TV, for instance. This, as I have argued in *Ordinary People and the Media*, reflects the changes in the manufacture of celebrity more generally, as the media have begun to 'produce celebrity on their own':

> Where once the media were more or less content to pick up celebrities produced through a range of sports, news and entertainment contexts, or to respond to approaches from publicists, promotions and public relations personnel, contemporary television in particular has introduced a much greater degree of vertical integration into the industrial structure which produces their celebrities. In addition to exploiting those who have already been established through other means, television has learnt that it can also invent, produce, market and sell on its celebrities from scratch – and on a much larger scale than ever before.
> (Turner, 2010: 15)

Overwhelmingly, this shift in the structure of production has resulted in the heightened participation of ordinary people in the media: the global success of reality TV formats – of all kinds, from *Big Brother*, *Idol* and *The Amazing Race* to *If You Are the One* or *Wife Swap* – has made ordinary people more visible across the whole of the mass media. Digital media's development of the capacity for ordinary people to create an online presence through 'life-streaming' and other strategies is also a major factor here, and then there is the rising tide of YouTube celebrities which bypasses the conventional gatekeepers for elite celebrity altogether.

As ordinary people have gained greater access to celebrity, the elite status of the celebrity – that is, their extraordinary dimension – has begun to break down. As a result, we now have what Grindstaff (2014) has called 'the ordinary celebrity'. In the representations of these celebrities, it is the ordinary which is by far the dominant discourse. While they may, for a time, enjoy the privileges (as well as the disadvantages) of the public visibility identified with the elite celebrity, it is overwhelmingly the performance of their 'ordinariness', itself carefully constructed, that defines their public identities. These identities are firmly embedded in the social, rather than abstracted from it: 'while professional celebrities can be constructed as "just like ordinary people" (only famous)' Grindstaff (2014) says, 'ordinary celebrities are constructed *as* ordinary people' (339). Young audiences relate to YouTube celebrities, Bednarski suggests, because many of these stars *are* just like them: 'students, living at home, buying stuff, playing games, hanging out, being awkward'. 'A large part of the charm of the YouTuber's videos', he continues, is 'that they are homemade. Literally, in the bedroom or in the basement' (Bednarski, 2015, np). As such comments imply, ordinary celebrity moves us closer to the social; as celebrity mutates from being an elite and magical condition to an almost reasonable expectation of everyday existence, it 'infiltrates' people's 'expectations of who they are and who they can be' (Grindstaff, 2014: 340). Couldry (2003) has framed celebrity as a discursive bridge between the world of the media and that of the everyday life of ordinary people; for the ordinary celebrity, at least for a time, that bridge is more than discursive.

This shift may matter. Probably the most uncompromising presentation of the case that it *does* matter, is found in Chris Rojek's (2012) *Fame Attack* which argues that the contemporary formation of celebrity, in which the ordinary celebrity is so pivotal, is popularising new and worrying social and cultural values. Rojek suggests that by 'colonising everyday life, by codifying personality and standardizing social control', fame may be affecting people in ways we do not fully comprehend: 'the costs of living in a culture in which social impact for the majority is out of reach, where commodified magnetism is frequently taken for charisma, and a sense of popular fraternization is mediated through commercialised para-social relationships', he says, 'are tricky to estimate' (184). Much of the public commentary on celebrity reflects similar concerns to those outlined in Rojek's book. Typically, it will point to the representations of particular individuals – Kim Kardashian, Justin Bieber, Lindsay Lohan or just about any member of the cast of *Jersey Shore* – and ask if the values and identities they popularise are serving our society well. When our television screens, magazines, news broadcasts and websites are littered with stories about the (mostly) young, extroverted, up-for-it, 'fun-loving', self-absorbed party animals who populate the key reality TV franchises and much of the news emanating from the popular music industry, one can understand why such concerns might be raised. When these individuals have been extracted from the everyday life that the rest of us are living, but will soon find themselves retrojected back into it, the discursive as well as the 'real life' boundaries between the world of celebrity and that of the everyday lives of ordinary people start to fracture – thus increasing the social provenance of the performance of the ordinary celebrity. Understandable though such public concerns might seem, however, it is also worth noting that their general tenor is entirely consistent with generations of elite, taste-based, reaction to popular cultural forms. The moral panics that regularly fill the very same media outlets which survive by promoting their celebrity content (Rowe, 2015) need to be taken with a least a few grains of salt. As a result, it is not surprising that there are a number of different assessments of this situation, and of the likely social consequences of a celebrity culture in which the ordinary celebrity is playing an increasingly prominent role. I want to look at some of these assessments in the following section by focusing on their discussions of reality TV.

Reacting to reality TV

It should go without saying that reality TV has achieved such prominence in television scheduling around the world that it can no longer be written off, as it was initially, as a passing phase. Even if many of the individual examples of the formats have gradually exhausted their appeal, there is no shortage of replacements. The key premise of reality TV– that audiences want to watch ordinary people perform themselves on screen – remains valid. It is inherent in the format that it can accommodate a particularly wide range of possible audience engagements. The kind of engagement each iteration of the format may seem to prefer will vary as well; while there are talent shows such as *American Idol* which happily humiliate the wannabe but talentless contestants, others such as *The Voice* generate a feel-good alignment with contestants who are explicitly selected for their musical talent. Partly as a consequence of their adaptability, as they are indigenised and tailored to particular locations and audiences, reality TV formats have been taken up around the globe. Everywhere they appear, they have demonstrated the capacity to generate high public profiles for individual participants and a cohort of contracted but disposable celebrity-commodities for the producers.

For the participants, it seems, what is on offer is more than just a period of celebrity or the possibility (slim, admittedly) of a career in the media. The achievement of media visibility, in itself, appears to be central, and personally validating – much in the way implied by Couldry's (2003) myth of the media centre. One of the notable findings to emerge from research which involves interviews with these participants is their view that the public exposure required to achieve that visibility is intrinsically valuable to them personally (Collins, 2008). Displaying and thus confirming their individual identities is regarded as a fundamental element in the process of their own self-fashioning and becoming (Andrejevic, 2004; Sender, 2012) – even though they have no control over how that process is represented on screen. As Banet-Weiser has argued in relation to self-branding more generally, such a commodification of the self somehow manages to present itself as a kind of authenticity: self-branding, she says, 'is seen not as an imposition of a concept or product by corporate culture but rather as the individual taking on the project herself as a way to access her "true" self' (Banet-Weiser, 2012: 61). Importantly too, for the ordinary celebrity, the successful production of this 'true self' cuts across a crucial set of cultural and social strata, significantly changing their status as they migrate from the non-media world into the 'social centre' (Couldry, 2003) of the media.

The core interest for me in this chapter, though, does not lie in what the ordinary person goes through as they learn how to perform themselves in public – or, indeed, in why they would do that. Rather, my interest is in how that performance is received, understood and used by those watching it – this, as a means of investigating how celebrity culture participates in everyday life. Quite some time ago, John Hartley described television as a tool for what he called 'transmodern teaching', with formats such as reality TV assisting in the formation of 'DIY citizenship' (Hartley, 1999). Hartley saw this as a positive, democratising, development of the capacities of popular media. There is a further development of that argument, made in many quarters now, which also proposes that reality TV has an especially strong and effective pedagogic mission, but that this mission is not really aimed at empowering its subjects. Rather, according to Hay and Ouelette's (2008) formulation, reality TV presents us with models of 'better living' that are aimed at teaching the individual how to fashion the self in accord with the needs of a neoliberal society. This proposes a very different politics of representation to that proposed by John Hartley, as Bev Skeggs and Helen Wood explain:

> Television [appears] to be offering lessons in individualization across our screens, exposing in numerous ways, from makeovers to game shows, incitements for 'ordinary' people to perform their own self-awareness, self-work and ultimately self-transformation, operating as a technology of governmentality, and making the self's value visible to others. It offered instructions to audiences which are useful in a current neo-liberal epoch where the motif of self-responsibility assists in the withdrawal of state support and in generating bodies ripe for the conditions of the flexible labour market. (Skeggs and Wood, 2012: 4)

It is one thing to locate this as a potential to be read from particular examples of the reality TV format, but it is another to demonstrate that it works that way on actual audiences. Indeed, much of the debate about the social function of reality TV is generated by readings of the texts themselves, with rather less in the way of research into how these texts are understood and/or appropriated into their audiences' everyday lives. However, it is the latter we need to understand better if we are to develop a stronger sense of the social function of this kind of programming and the versions of personhood it appears to recommend.

One example of such work, which has the potential to complicate our understanding of the pedagogic functions of reality TV, comes from Bev Skeggs and Helen Wood. While they acknowledge the theoretical possibility that television can indeed operate as a 'technology of governmentality' and in many ways their work supports that as the default principle, their research project in *Reacting to Reality TV* (Skeggs and Wood, 2012) is designed to test whether it is quite that straightforward in practice. They set out to discover how television audiences react to what they agree looks like a very clear pedagogic project outlined in the reality TV series, *Wife Swap*, in which the wives/mothers from two ordinary families from contrasting locations on (usually) the class spectrum swap places for a period of two weeks. The show deliberately both exploits and complicates stereotypes of class, gender and race through set-ups that are guaranteed to generate conflict as well as, occasionally, result in the generation of more tolerant or flexible responses from the participants. The conflicts are the more entertaining, of course, and are often quite spectacular, with high levels of emotion involved; such moments are among the engines of the format. As is the case with most television formats using ordinary people, the performances in the texts allow quite a bit of room for varied responses from viewers; it can be just as entertaining to deplore what is happening on screen as to applaud it, or indeed to learn from it.

For their research, Skeggs and Wood interviewed groups of subjects but they also sat with them and recorded their reactions and conversations as they watched the programme. The choice of the word 'react' differentiates Skeggs and Wood's approach from more conventional versions of audience studies which tend to focus on the interpretation of a text; here, the emphasis is on what their subjects' immediate verbal and physical reactions, and their interactions, told the researchers about the social relations between audiences and television. Significantly, I think, the conversations among the viewers of *Wife Swap* that Skeggs and Wood studied were not just about their interpretation of these media representations, even though they were clearly quite strongly engaged by the programme. The conversations were also to do with calibrating the relation between what the audience members perceived as the politics or ethics of what Skeggs and Wood describe as the 'performances of personhood' they saw on screen, and the domestic practices they entailed, on the one hand, and the social norms, everyday practices and contexts the viewers inhabited themselves, on the other. Skeggs and Wood describe this as an engagement in the 'tournaments of value' (233) that took place amongst their viewers as they watched. The phrase highlights the ethical intensity of what is said as audience members actively evaluate the performances of personhood they see on television against their own social experience and cultural identities. These tournaments of value take place in contexts which are already thoroughly (often highly explicitly) classed and gendered, of course, and it is important to emphasise the fact that Skeggs and Wood's research suggests that these factors continue to maintain their power to overdetermine how these audiences react to what they see.

This research speaks directly to the concerns noted at the beginning of this chapter that, through reality TV and its promotion of a particular kind of ordinary celebrity, television is popularising ways of behaving that do not serve society well. According to such concerns, it is of little comfort that such behaviours might be exposed by the formats in question as vulgar, ignorant or unsophisticated, from the perspective of a relatively conventional middle-class critique (something that occurs in *Wife Swap* and would appear to be the premise of many examples of the reality format, such as, for instance, *From Ladette to Lady*). This is because the behaviours that are the subject of this critique are often represented as the most authentic, the most entertaining, and therefore, it is feared, for some members of the audience, the most attractive. Since the participants in reality TV are selected for their capacity to perform their ordinariness in as compelling and entertaining a manner as possible, albeit in varying ways, there is a concern that the power of their performance encourages the viewer to accept or even to endorse their behaviours. There seems little doubt that the appeal of a format such as *Wife Swap* (and many others, from the more benign makeover formats to the various versions of *The Real Housewives*) must lie equally in its capacity to exploit the spectacle of the participants' resistance to acquiring the recommended forms of social sophistication as in demonstrating their need of it. However, given the fact that such a text easily allows for either (or both) kinds of reading, it is difficult to find a way of generating evidence that might tell us something conclusive about its social function, from only examining it as a set of representations.

Consequently, Skeggs and Wood choose to move away from analytic approaches that are, as they put it, 'structured through the traditional politics of representation' (38). Instead, Skeggs and Wood suggest a different focus – in effect, on the observable social interactions around the text as a community of viewers engages with it. They adopt Jack Bratich's (2007) suggestion that it would be more accurate to describe the social and cultural function of reality TV as having more to do with 'intervention than representation'; at its most active, he says, reality TV does not merely '*represent* the present conjuncture – it *interjects itself* into the conjuncture' (7). While this is a concept that would benefit from more development, it does reorient the problem in suggestive ways. It proposes that reality TV programmes, rather than having an 'effect' on the social, and in many ways as a result of the perceived 'ordinariness' of the participants, become *part of* the social as viewers react to them.

Viewed in terms of what it can tell us about the social consequences of reality TV, the evidence produced by this work carries both positive and negative implications. However, what is most valuable about Skeggs and Wood's politically nuanced and empirically detailed research is that it demonstrates the complexity of the ways in which television might intervene in the social, and thus works to counteract, or at the very least to significantly complicate, concerns about the vulnerability of audiences to the wholesale incorporation of the attractions and values of celebrity culture as transmitted via the media.

However, that said, there is also evidence from other researchers which points, perhaps just as clearly, the other way: that is, towards moments where we witness what appears to be the demonstration of celebrity culture's effective integration into the practices and expectations of everyday life. There are now numbers of studies which find that young people, in particular, regard fame as itself a realistic life ambition and unapologetically aspire to it (Turner, 2014b). Celebrities, according to industry research reported in Bednarski (2015), are especially influential on young people, aged between 13 and 24; YouTubers, in particular, are regarded as 'aspirational: meaning that they have traits youth strive to achieve: someone I look up to/I respect/I'd like to be, does the things I want to do' (2015, np). Such an aspiration generates the large numbers of hopefuls who audition for casting in the big reality franchises and who must master the appropriate performance of personhood in order to be successful. It is an indication of the scale of the phenomenon of ordinary celebrity to note that this is not an entirely unrealistic ambition. The promise of celebrity is underwritten by the numerous instances where the ordinary individual – through reality TV, through YouTube or through personal websites or blogs – has actually fulfilled that ambition. There is also the research noted earlier in which interviews with participants reveal that the aspiration of achieving a media presence is readily integrated into a process of self-fashioning and personal affirmation (Andrejevic, 2004).

There is a growing body of work which employs a variety of disciplinary and methodological approaches to focus on specific reality TV programmes and genres which seem, on the face of it, to depend upon the successful promulgation of a version of selfhood in which the discursive frames of, and the versions of personhood identified with, celebrity are directly implicated. Among the more nuanced and sophisticated examples are studies of makeover television (Weber, 2009; Taylor, 2011; Sender, 2012). Makeover formats are key sites for the ambiguities noted earlier in this book – where participation simultaneously, and inherently, carries the dual potential for empowerment and exploitation. There is the perceived benefit to the individual of the makeover, and with it perhaps some of the benefits of achieving even a short-term experience of media celebrity. There is also the benefit of going through this experience publicly, through the media, in order to put it on display as an authentic performance of the self. On the other hand, however, there is what might be described as a ritual of abjection as the individual performs their desire for change, a performance the format requires as a narrative necessity before they can begin the makeover process. And, more fundamentally, while there will certainly be a strong argument made for the empowerment inherent in the subject's choosing to make themselves over, there is also the matter of the significant ideological work required to produce the eventual presentation of a particular kind of gendered social self that, putatively (we might imagine, but we do not know), plays out in the everyday as well as on the screen. The politics implicated in the production of that mediated self, as Brenda Weber has argued, are full of contradictions. In her discussion of one participant in *Extreme Makeover*, she points out, this woman's 'newfound beauty', notwithstanding the concerns we might have about the ruthlessness of the cultural politics that led her to seek the intervention that produced it, actually '*does* increase her cultural power' (Weber, 2014: 370): 'by capitulating to social standards about appearance', Weber says, 'Amy has become empowered to transcend those very standards' (369). At such points, reality TV appears to have successfully managed its integration into the processes of self-fashioning available to us in our everyday lives, but the implications of that integration are certainly complicated. For the person directly involved as the subject of the makeover, there is every possibility, as Brenda Weber acknowledges, that it constitutes a worthwhile, even empowering, experience. In terms of what such formats teach us about the process of constructing a cultural identity, about the role of the media and media visibility in such a process, and, in the end, what kinds of cultural identities we should desire in the first place, it may be a little more worrying.

These focused pieces of research are mounting in volume and sophistication, and one wonders whether we will reach a point when there will be a sufficient body of evidence for us to be able to start claiming to know, much better than we do now, precisely how celebrity culture intervenes in the social through reality TV – both for those who are active participants in it and for those who consume and react to it. My sense is that, as these studies are mounting up, there is a growing unease, not only within society at large but more specifically within media and cultural studies, about the values, assumptions and behaviours these formats appear to prefer and thus to recommend, and which may well motivate those who wish to become participants. We don't hear much about DIY citizenship anymore, but we hear a lot about exploitation. However, there is a potential danger in simply aggregating such studies in a manner that cumulatively pathologises the behaviours in question; it is all too easy to stigmatise the participants rather than determine, on the one hand, whose interests are actually served by the production of celebrity through reality TV, or, on the other hand, to incorporate our recognition of just how socially grounded are the actual processes of consumption. Some of the subjects in Skeggs and Wood's study clearly resent what they easily decode as middle-class pedagogy in the representations of the participants on screen in *Wife Swap*. Their reaction implicitly endorses those participants who defy the programme's pedagogic mission (and there are plenty of these) by unrepentantly adopting modes of performance and display that transgress the norms being recommended. Once again, the challenge is not to foreclose the possibility that something like this might be productive, while investigating the consequences when a celebrity culture that so thoroughly serves the commercial interests of the media is integrated into the social.

What is worth noting, however, is that when we move beyond Western contexts of consumption, there is a much less ambiguous view on how celebrity culture intervenes into the social – perhaps because the values and ideologies underpinning celebrity are thrown into sharper relief when removed from their original cultural context. The centrality of the focus on the construction of the individual is one key element that runs against the grain of some of the more communal value systems in place outside the West. Celebrity is hardwired into notions of individualism and, as Robert van Krieken points out, 'the more communal the sense of self is', the less interest there will be in 'attaching recognition or esteem to particular individuals'; while 'the more individualistic social and cultural life is, the more likely it is that it will generate a more expansive network of celebrities' (van Krieken, 2012: 24). Research on reality TV in Asia (Keane, Fung and Moran, 2007; Edwards and Jeffries, 2010) and the Middle East (Kraidy, 2010; Sakr, 2007) is producing accounts of instances where the successful take-up of reality TV formats, and their consequent construction of forms of celebrity around the participants, have created significant concerns. Of course, in many if not most locations outside the West, the adaptation of these formats is charged with a highly political valence. To their critics, the formats are not harmless entertainments; rather, they are regarded as intervening into long-established ways of life by undermining or competing with them, and thus generating alarm at the possible cultural or social change they might motivate.

Celebrity, as a personal aspiration for the individual and as a recommended means of achieving social status in a mediated culture, is a target of such criticism because it is so often seen as one of the most influential media vehicles driving cultural and social change. Typically, in the response to the cultural influence of celebrity, there is concern about the perceived incompatibility between the values embedded in the character of the performances required of the participants of reality TV and the traditional values of the community. Earlier I referred to Jamilah Maliki's (2008) research into the controversy around the Malaysian talent programme, *Akademi Fantasia*, which was seen as smuggling in Western values that were both socially and religiously unacceptable. In an example from Bangladesh, Din Mohammed (2012) has discussed the development of an *Idol*-like television talent contest, which was inspired by the popular music circulating informally rather than commercially among Dhaka's urban poor. The contest was open only to those who drove the Tin Chakas or 'three-wheelers' in the city and this proved to be a highly attractive element for audiences. As the programme's commercial potential was recognised and exploited, and as the successful contestants achieved celebrity status, both the programme and the contestants' relation to the community whose music it had set out to promote became increasingly strained. Mohammed documents reaction to the negative effects of the commercialisation of what had started out as a community enterprise, as well as to the limited personal benefits and significant personal costs that resulted from the short-lived celebrity achieved through the programme.

The communities referred to in these accounts appear to have no doubt that reality TV has the capacity to intervene in the social, that celebrity is a key means through which this occurs, and that it does so in order to serve the interests of the media, rather than those of the community. We are less categoric in our assessment of the role of reality TV in the West, in part, perhaps, due to the scale and richness of the research in the field and the conflicting patterns of evidence it has produced. However, there is work emerging on another media platform in the West where some of the judgements do seem to be unequivocal and well supported. This is research which directly addresses the role of celebrity culture in supplying the discursive repertoire, as well as the value system, for the ordinary person's construction of a public presence online.

Celebrity, status and a presence online

As I have already noted at various points in this book, the development of user-generated content (UGC) online has become one of the most talked-about dimensions of the re-invented media. The heartland of online celebrity culture – the world of microblogs, personal websites and social media such as Twitter, Instagram and Facebook – shares the online space with, among other things, news blogs and activist sites that are very much motivated by some kind of collectivist principle: supporting a particular cause or otherwise seeking to use the media for an intervention of a quite different kind to those discussed in this chapter (Howley, 2013). It is this kind of intervention, however, that is among the reasons why the development of UGC capacities was so enthusiastically welcomed as a new means of constructing community and redistributing power. The affordances of digital media enabled such groups to create networked publics, at little or no cost, and without dealing with the gatekeepers of the mass media, in order to 'rally support for politics or events that are important to individuals' for reasons that go 'far beyond self-image' (Banet-Weiser, 2012: 88). However, as Banet-Weiser goes on to say, this collective dimension of the online world has also existed 'in constant tension' with quite contradictory 'individualising tendencies' (ibid.) A core expression of these tendencies is the construction of the personal web presence. We live in a 'media society that often equates social power with visibility', but as we have seen in the commodification of the participants in reality television, it 'is a limited visibility' that works to 'commodify identities within boundaries established by the communications industries' (Banet-Weiser, 2012: 35). As an instance of the functioning of those boundaries, within the blogosphere as well as across social media such as Facebook and Twitter, celebrity has become a widely adopted generic frame as well as a motivation for the public, and indeed also for the private, performance of the self.

In her investigation of the cultural production of social status via social media among workers in the 'tech scene' in California, Alice Marwick found that social media's 'broadcasting ability' had transformed the practices associated with the establishment of social status among that group, encouraging people to 'prioritize attention and visibility' as they constructed themselves as the 'micro-celebrities' we have discussed earlier in this book (Marwick, 2013: 10). Within the world her research subjects inhabited, she suggests, a high status online was the product of successful self-branding strategies and it had 'tangible effects on face-to-face interactions': it opened doors, and blurred 'the lines between cultural, social and financial capital' (ibid.). Marwick argues that this is directly related to the affordances of Web 2.0:

> Web 2.0 is a neoliberal technology of subjectivity that teaches users how to succeed in postmodern American consumer capitalism. Social media not only demonstrates the lessons of white-collar business success by rewarding flexibility, entrepreneurialism, and risk-taking; it also provides a blueprint of how to prosper in a society where social status is predicated on the cultural logic of celebrity. (14)

In her more general discussion of life-streaming, Banet-Weiser also connects the focus on individualisation and self-branding to the technologies in use, pointing out that digital technologies are overwhelmingly about the representation of the self to others, and citing research that talks of social media contributing to a 'culture of celebrity, materialism and entitlement' (Banet-Weiser, 2012: 87). 'Narcissism', she says, 'is part of the very structure of online technologies', but this is masked by the fact that it has been effectively de-pathologised by being 'reimagined within the context of self-branding and social media not only as a moral duty to oneself but also as a kind of business model' (88). Marwick similarly found that 'blatant self-promotion is now stock in trade not only for up and coming rap stars and actresses, but also for software developers, journalists and academics. Creating a public presence has become a required part of securing and maintaining a job' (Marwick, 2013: 161). It is ironic that the very technologies that were supposed to release so much democratising potential have been so effectively harnessed to generate new modes of individualisation, new kinds of commodity and new markers of distinction, just as readily as new forms of community.

Marwick nominates the key discursive coordinates of what she describes as the 'cultural logic' of celebrity: in which the 'highest value is given to mediation, visibility and attention' (14). These closely accord with the coordinates nominated within a very different kind of analysis in van Kreiken's (2012) *Celebrity Society*; there, he argues that 'celebrity society' is organised around the 'distribution of visibility, attention, and recognition' (4). And again, there are similar reference points nominated in Olivier Driessens' discussion of the 'celebritisation of society'. The factors he describes as the most active in 'moulding' this celebritised society are 'mediatisation, personalisation, and commodification' (Driessens, 2013: 649–653). The similarities between these accounts constitute a reasonable consensus on what we might think of as the discursive repertoire for the ways in which celebrity culture, generally, exercises a shaping influence on society; that is, through allocating high social status to a mediated visibility that generates public attention for the individual, and through attributing cultural value to that attention and the recognition that comes with it.

Driessens describes the rise of celebrity culture as a long-term structural development, or a 'meta-process' like globalisation. Rather than locating celebrity's social and cultural prominence as the outcome of a process through which the mass media directly shapes the social, he locates celebrity within a broader, less direct and explicitly mediatised context:

> Importantly, this stress on mediatisation instead of the (mass) media urges us to rethink the role of the media and to broaden our focus from the media as technological platforms or content providers and ideological apparatuses to an understanding that pays attention to not only the direct involvement of the media industries and their products (magazines, movies, television shows etc.) but also their indirect roles as they actively co-shape our social environment and (non) media-related practice, an analytic approach which is promoted by mediatisation studies. (653)

Consistent with the approach to mediatisation I outlined in Chapter 1, Driessens focuses on how 'celebrity moulds the cultures we live in' as well as on 'what its consequences are, for instance, in terms of power relations, expectations, identity formation and self-presentation' (653). This takes us from talking about celebrity as a discrete formation, and towards thinking about celebrity culture as a mediatised repertoire of discourses and values.

As Marwick shows us, celebrity culture concentrates these discourses and values around the performance of the self, which, much as Skeggs and Wood demonstrate, is then culturally evaluated. For Marwick, what emerges from the micro-celebrities she investigates is how they have internalised the culture's proscription of the desired self – typically performed, she argues, as the ideal, neoliberal subject:

> This ideal subject appears in many locations. She is present in makeover shows like *What Not to Wear* and *Queer Eye for the Straight Guy* which contrast an undesirable 'before' with a consumer-friendly 'after'. He can be seen in reality television, which presents individuals as products (celebrities) and normalises corporate and government surveillance. And she is apparent in Web 2.0 technologies, which idealize and reward a particular persona: highly visible, entrepreneurial, and self-configured to be watched and consumed by others.
> (Marwick, 2013: 13)

Marwick's observations refer, of course, to what is only one relatively enclosed, but nonetheless expanding, component of the re-invented media. However, research on this component provides us with a substantial body of evidence about how celebrity culture intervenes in the social, and what seem to be the consequences of that intervention. When we examine the proliferation of the micro-celebrity, of life-streaming, and more generally the integration of self-branding into the production of identity, it does indeed seem as if the media is operating, as Driessens says, as a cross-field meta-process that is shaping, translating and, in the broadest sense, *authoring* identities. As such, it is inculcating celebrity culture through its successful privileging of media visibility not only as a mode of authenticity but also as a producer of distinction, and through the way the media's pre-eminent role of attracting public attention has extended into the realm of the private and the personal as well.

Conclusion

While Driessens' deployment of the notion of mediatisation is useful, it remains quite difficult to make detailed arguments about the consequences of celebrity culture which move us beyond what has become the comparatively comfortable territory of representation and interpretation. The spectre of crude effects models looms, or the taste-based moral panics that have accompanied virtually every interesting development in media culture in the last 50 years. And yet the hints about celebrity generating significant social and cultural consequences are certainly there; from my point of view, most persuasively, in the accounts of non-Western responses to the adaptation of Western formats for reality TV and their cultural valorisation of the ordinary celebrity. Jack Bratich's (2007) suggestion that the media – in the case of reality TV formats, or more broadly the culture that has developed around the ordinary celebrity – 'intervenes' in the social is helpful because it does take us beyond merely reading representations for their likely meanings and directs us to a closer focus on what happens when representations transition into playing a role within ordinary people's experience of everyday life. We still know very little about this, however. The possibility that celebrity's ubiquity and pervasiveness, and its more recent infiltration into ordinary people's everyday lives, does carry social consequences constitutes a powerful argument for more detailed empirical research aimed at generating evidence that will help us better understand the social functions of celebrity culture into the future.

At the same time, it is important to keep in mind an argument that I have been making throughout this book, that much of what is most significant about the re-invented media has its roots in the commercial interests of media organisations. Celebrity culture is not some autochthonous development organically emerging from 'the people'; this is a product of an increasingly commercialised, concentrated and powerful media in a world where the media increasingly shape our lives and what we think about them. While there are certainly perspectives from which the rise of the ordinary celebrity and the demoticisation of celebrity culture might be regarded positively, and perhaps I have underplayed that here, it is also worth heeding Driessens' warning: 'we should not be dazzled', he says, 'by the seemingly diverse and democratic character of celebrity; rather we should pay attention to how and by whom it is produced' (Driessens, 2013: 646). If anything, celebrity culture's pervasiveness makes this kind of scrutiny more important than ever before. As Couldry has commented in relation to the commodification of the self that has become so fundamental to celebrity culture, 'the more we desire to be visible in media across all domains, the more vulnerable to a currently unaccountable form of power – media's symbolic power – all domains of social action become' (Couldry, 2012: 207–208).

Notes

1 Cited as an epigraph, this has no publication details, but the references to Bernays in Rojek's bibliography are to works published from the late 1920s through to the later 1940s.
2 This is much less common now in most of the fields where celebrity is prominent, with the significant exception of sport, where the idea persists that the sports star has a responsibility to appropriately serve as a role model for young people (Whannel, 2002).

CONCLUSION

Teaching the re-invented media

In this final chapter I want to present some conclusions – initially by way of a summary account of what the re-invented media has become. I then want to use the arguments made in this book as a perspective from which to voice some personal opinions about the current state of the teaching of the media in our universities. In particular, I am concerned about an emerging division between the teaching of the traditional mass media – television, radio, print, sometimes advertising or film – and the teaching of new media, variously described in programme prospectuses as new media, digital media, social media or multi-platform media. While it is not hard to see how the foregrounding of the most recent developments in the media would place these latter teaching programmes at the cutting edge of media studies and would thus serve as an effective attractor to potential students, it is harder to see the academic benefit of such a bifurcation of the field. If we set the marketing objectives for the respective programmes aside, and if we accept that the mid-2000s hype about the potential of new media platforms to replace traditional media was overblown, there is little to justify such a division. It does not reflect a division in the relevant industries nor in their political economies; it does not reflect the practices of audiences which are increasingly hybridised and platform-agnostic; and it does not reflect the location of media content which is now notoriously mobile and rarely platform-specific in its distribution. It does reflect, however, a limited view of media history by foregrounding disruptions over continuities, displacement over persistence, technologies over society. Most importantly, in my view, this division carries the danger of effectively relegating the analysis of media power to the status of a second-order issue. In my discussion of the teaching of the media, therefore, I want to make some suggestions about what a more inclusive approach might look like, an approach interested in accommodating the *whole* of the mediascape, before offering some concluding thoughts on the implications of this book's account of the contemporary media.

The re-invented media: what has it become?

First, however, what are the core components of the re-invented media? As outlined in the previous chapters, they include the fact that we are no longer dealing with the mass media alone and that so many of the new platforms are networked in their structure and hybridised in their patterns of use; that much of the media now identify as commercial organisations rather than cultural institutions; that this latter shift has resulted in the dominance of entertainment over information in media content; that the relation between the media and the nation-state, far from being irrelevant, is becoming both more politically contingent and increasingly important, even while the capacities of regulatory policy regimes seem to have been outstripped by the scale and pace of technological change; that the media's engagement with the production of identities and its intervention into the practices and the values of everyday life has been dramatically enhanced by the growth of celebrity culture; and finally, it is becoming more difficult to distinguish between the practices of media consumption and practices connected to other domains of everyday life as our cultures become progressively more mediatised.

The first of these components takes us back to the focus of Chapter 1, the decline of the mass media paradigm, and the development of narrowcast, networked, mobile and social media. It is important to emphasise that these categories, while useful for analytical purposes, are not mutually exclusive. What might seem to be boundaries between them are in fact quite porous; while they might involve discrete technologies, they are linked through their content and their users as well as, often, through the corporate structures, as well as the communications infrastructures, within which they operate. 'Private' thoughts circulated to followers on Twitter or to friends on Facebook can easily end up being circulated to a mass audience via other media users and platforms, with or without the consent of the producer of the original content. Rather than dealing with the mass media and social media as if they were separate and distinct domains, then, it would make more sense to think of the re-invented media as composed of a complex repertoire of interlinked and interoperable capacities, situated variously along a continuum that takes us from the mass media at the most definitively public end, to networked media as the most hybridised formation, and then to social media at the most personal or private end.

It would also make sense to take José van Dijck's advice and adopt another term for what is now usually called 'social media', partly because this term tends to be used quite loosely to refer to a wider range of networked media than the term 'social' can really justify. van Dijck, though, also has reservations about the appropriateness of the term, 'social', itself. Noting how many of the key terms within the world of social media (e.g. 'friends', 'collaboration') resonate with the 'communalist jargon of early utopian visions of the Web as a space that inherently enhances social activity', van Dijck goes on to point out that the reality is a little different, and that this needs to be reflected in the terminology we use:

> In reality, the meanings of these words have increasingly been informed by automated technologies that direct human sociality. Therefore, the term

'connective media' would be preferable over 'social media'. What is deemed to be 'social' is in fact the result of human input shaped by computed input and vice versa – a sociotechnical ensemble whose components can hardly be told apart. (van Dijck, 2013: 13–14)

I am persuaded by this. 'Connective' media is more accurate as a means of describing the capacities concerned, but it also has the benefit of disarticulating these capacities from a term that implies a degree of community or sociality that serves to recommend them as if they were uncomplicatedly serving 'us', rather than also working, in their hybridised fashion, in the service of interests that have nothing to do with 'us' at all.

The hybridity of the actual patterns of contemporary media use has been under-examined, perhaps as a consequence of media studies' preferred focus on convergence, but, as I argue in Chapter 1, hybridity does seem to me to be a key attribute of the re-invented media and it needs to be used more actively to organise analysis. It helps to refocus attention on the social or cultural functions, rather than just the technological drivers, of media use. As Madaniou and Miller (2013) demonstrate, the choices users make between platforms, media and applications are in the first instance driven by social, cultural and personal considerations, and are only subsequently to do with the capacities of the technologies themselves. Admittedly, hybridisation makes my suggestion of a media continuum more of a heuristic device than a practicality, perhaps, but the media continuum still has the advantage of enabling us to think more inclusively, with all the components of the re-invented media participating in an overarching interface, each in their own particular ways.

A constant theme running through this book has been the growth in the commercialisation of the media's institutional and industrial structures as well as the marketisation of its activities across regional, national and local operating environments. The effects of this are far-reaching. They include the commercial media's prioritisation of the production of entertainment rather than information, as well as the related transformation of what remains of the commitment to the provision of information: the 'crisis in journalism', and the gradual corporatisation and enclosure of the internet. Even much of connective media, one might have thought among the least likely media platforms to be captured by the market, is now tightly articulated to the commercial practices of targeted marketing, consumer profiling and the commodification and sale of personal data. Sociality itself has been commodified online – van Dijck (2013: 14) describes the Facebook mission as 'making the social saleable' – and as we saw in Chapter 6, discourses of branding and celebrity are now framing personal practices of self-fashioning and self-presentation. At the level of the nation-state, the construction of national identity in many locations has also become a commercial exercise in branding, driven by the twin imperatives of modernisation and marketisation in a context of economic globalisation. Where once we might have assumed these were the imperatives which, when connected to the establishment of a liberal media, might lead towards the development of a liberal-democratic public sphere, that now seems far more dubious. As we saw in

Chapter 3, assumptions about the connection between the forces of marketisation and the principles of a liberal democracy need to be examined against the varying histories outside the West of what is now a politically diverse set of relationships between the media and the nation-state.

The de-Westernisation of media studies (Curran and Park, 2000) may still have some way to go, but media studies in the West is becoming more aware of the diversity of media systems around the globe – and that this diversity is constitutive, rather than just a passing phase in the inevitable evolution of 'their' systems to become just like 'ours' as globalisation kicks in. Pleasingly, we have moved beyond an assumption, implicit in much earlier work on television as well as on media cultures in general, that a focus upon the West or upon the leading nations in Anglophone media studies would be enough to enable us to properly understand the function of the media, wherever it operates. We are rediscovering the power of specific historic, cultural and political conditions to shape how the media is structured, how it is consumed, how it operates, and in whose interests. The work of pioneers of a more nuanced global perspective within Anglophone media studies (Curtin, 2004, 2007; Tinic, 2005; Straubhaar, 2007) plays its part in this, but it is also a reflection of the increasing visibility of the other side to the coin of globalisation – the fragmentation of markets and the development of local industries focused upon their own communities. The internationalisation of media studies in general – in terms of publishing, conferences and the like – has resulted in those working in media studies in the West becoming much more open to, and interested in, attending to media research located in different parts of the world than previously. As a result, we are better placed, because better informed, to recognise the social and political contingency of the function of the media wherever it is located. This account of the re-invented media, therefore, incorporates that recognition, and its awareness of the global diversity of media systems. As an outcome of that recognition, and as I have argued in Chapter 3, there is a need to engage in a much more informed way with the ongoing reconfiguration of the relations between the media and the state in the current era. The reconfiguration of this relationship is driven by the complex of conditions around state investment in modernisation, the associated forms of cultural liberalisation, the commercialisation of these processes and the media's participation in them, and subsequently the growing influence of the media on the construction of national identities for international consumption. The work on nation-branding in the post-socialist states (Kaneva, 2012) and commercial nationalism in the former Yugoslavia (Volcic and Andrejevic, 2015), that I have cited a number of times in this book, are notable examples of highly localised and closely historicised analysis that is moving into the mainstream of our accounts of what the media is becoming and how its commercial power is being deployed in new, socially transformative but politically diverse, ways.

At a number of points in this book, I have expressed the view that media, communications and cultural studies have allowed the issue of media power to be backburnered in recent years. It is critically important to recognise that the arrangement of media power, the interests it serves, and the range of areas upon which it is deployed, have all undergone significant change as the media has re-invented itself. As I argued in Part I of this book, the media no longer simply mediates between the public and other locations of power; it has its own interests to advance and these are overwhelmingly commercial. This does not mean that their activities are without political or social effects; indeed, in some contexts, that may be their clear intention. In most other contexts, however, any such effects are more likely to be collateral damage, a careless by-product of their concentrated pursuit of their own commercial interests. There is a similar story to tell in relation to the media's participation in the production of cultural identities for the individual. As we saw in the discussion of celebrity culture in Chapters 5 and 6, the media has taken on a more active role as the author or translator of cultural identities — hence the widespread and varied concerns about the production of personal and cultural identities through a television format such as reality TV, and through the cultural pervasiveness of the discourses and values of celebrity that Rojek (2012: 184) has described as 'colonising everyday life'. Again, these are more likely to be the accidental by-products of the media's primary activities than the outcome of deliberate strategies of social and political intervention. There is little comfort to be found in that, however, and Rojek is right to point to the significant gaps in our understanding of what the social consequences of celebrity culture might be.

This is far from being the only dimension of the re-invented media that we don't properly understand. As a consequence of the gradual marketisation of the internet, a whole new domain of media power has opened up by way of the monetisation of consumers' activity online, and the expansion in the commercial deployment of mechanisms for the monitoring and surveillance of consumer behaviour. Media use has been commodified in new and largely invisible ways, over which media users have little control and which, as we saw in Chapter 2, carry the potential for generating quite profound social and political consequences (Sunstein, 2009). Paradoxically, as we are moving away from the era of mass media — an era when the media were regarded as possessing too much, and overly concentrated, power — and supposedly towards an era in which there is some devolution of power to 'the people formerly known as the audience' (Rosen, 2006), we are actually experiencing what is a largely unregulated expansion and commercially driven diversification of the locations and sources of media power. As we saw in Chapter 4, regulation has fallen out of favour as a field of policy, or has lost the capacity to deal with the pace of change shaping the media landscape, and so the availability of public mechanisms to assist 'the people formerly known as the audience' to protect their interests is shrinking, even as the media extends its influence ever further into the practices of our everyday lives. This major rearrangement of media power looms as the most pressing concern for the next generation of media studies teaching and research. Unless we do better at integrating that concern, and in relation to all of the media domains to which it refers, within the broad range of what we consider as the objects of media studies, we will become irrelevant as a critical academic enterprise.

TV studies, new media studies and the divided curriculum

What are the implications of all this, then, for the teaching of media studies today? What follows in this section, I admit, is more opinionated than what has preceded it, but it does draw directly upon the arguments outlined in this book. I will start to address this question by spending a little time on the divided curriculum of contemporary media studies – roughly speaking, the widening gap between traditional media studies and what David Gauntlett (2007) famously labelled Media Studies 2.0. Typically, this gap is marked by the assumption that the age of traditional media – especially television – is over, and that the online environment is poised to become the dominant location for media distribution and consumption, and even in some cases media production. The gap is further marked by a distinction between the kind of 'passive' consumption assumed to take place in front of a television and the interactivity typically identified through reference to user-generated content online. Informed by students' own patterns of consumption, which tend to confirm the scenario used to support this version of the current state of the media, it is a highly seductive and so far successful way of generating demand for programmes in new media studies and the like. Even though, as I have argued at many points throughout this book, I do not believe this scenario, as a broad description of the current situation, is sustained by the evidence, I do sympathise with those who have taken it up as a way of maintaining the relevance and appeal of media and cultural studies programmes in the competitive environment of the contemporary university. The highly fashionable status of new media amongst our students, their familiarity with its use, and the corresponding trend towards disinterest in so-called 'heritage' or 'legacy' media, has made the teaching of an inclusive and historically informed media programme in the university genuinely more difficult.

Nonetheless, it is also the case that, to some extent, contemporary media and cultural studies have been complicit in creating this situation. With what has become in some quarters almost a default setting of a 'gee-whizz' alertness to the 'next big thing' – from cult television to the latest mobile app – as well as weakening incentives towards historicisation, media studies in particular has allowed its enthusiasm for new technologies, new platforms and new applications to dominate its research focus as well as what gets taught in its classes. It is important we do not lose sight of the various larger contexts (the social, the market, the nation, or shifts in the media's political economies) within which each innovation will have to find its place. Unfortunately, I think we are seeing signs of this happening now, as the pace of change continues to accelerate, and as the new products and possibilities offered up almost daily are endlessly distracting. As media platforms and products proliferate, it has become more difficult to teach the media – indeed to conceptualise the media – through one coherent and interrelated set of approaches; hence, the common pedagogic strategy of approaching the media as an anthology of affordances arranged in hierarchies of timeliness and popularity.

The lack of a conceptual frame for the re-invented media is precisely the problem that has motivated the writing of this book, but even so it is disturbing to see the extent to which so many examples of the media studies curriculum have tended to opt either for a focus on contemporary digital and multi-platform media or for a focus on more traditional mass media such as television. We should be dealing with *all* of them, just as our societies do, and in ways that show how the interface between them is structured and used.

I am less tolerant of the tendency within so much of new media studies, and in the related field of creative industries, for predicting the future. There are whole books on new media which are devoted to predicting the future of the media on the basis of anecdotal evidence and self-serving industry spin from the entrepreneurs of cool capitalism. Futurism has become far too comfortably embedded in this sub-disciplinary field. This is not because such activity has a record of getting its predictions right. James Curran (2011) has examined the 'long tradition of millenarian prophecy' in relation to new media technologies; examples he cites include the prediction that the camcorder would democratise television and that CD-ROMs would transform publishing. He goes on to present a series of case studies which compare the futurists' predictions with what actually happened in relation to four significant media developments over the last 30 years in the UK: cable television, interactive digital television, local community television and the dotcom boom. After demonstrating the folly of these predictions, Curran goes on to offer some explanations for their currency and impact, as well as for the uncritical response the predictions received from journalists. What, he asks, could account for these journalists having such a 'blind spot'? Key factors he cites include the supply of 'misinformation about the new media' which was 'in every instance', provided by 'the business interests promoting them'; the misjudgement of senior politicians keen to support the 'development of the "new information economy" as a way of offsetting the decline of the manufacturing sector'; and experts from the universities who 'talked up the impact of new media developments' (Curran, 2011: 104–105). The last of these, of course, includes the rhetoric of the new media futurists which fitted perfectly with the prevailing news values: 'articles about how new media will change how people live … were well suited to filling the expanding space devoted to consumer and lifestyle issues' (106). Curran points out the consequences of this combination of misinformation, political opportunism and the symbiosis of industry and academic hype: some of these predictions unwittingly played into the hands of a deregulatory government and so contributed to significant, arguably ill-advised, changes to the structure of the British media:

> A cumulative impression was cultivated over three decades that television was about to be so transformed that legislative safeguards protecting programme quality and diversity were less called for. During this period, television deregulation took place in Britain on a much greater scale than in most other northern European countries. This was aided by the way in which the future was enlisted to change the present. (110)

My point here is that this field of academic research and expertise should not behave as if it were engaged in a competitive game of trendspotting; it should not be exempt from the usual rules of evidence and argument that authorise academic analysis, no matter how 'cool' it feels to be on the inside of a new technological development. Getting this stuff wrong matters, and it is not something a reputable field of research should risk doing.

This bears on the uncomfortable fact that one of the key influences on such work can only be described as that of fashion. All disciplines are subject to intellectual fashions, of course, but rarely are they hitched up to such exorbitantly fashion-driven vehicles as the media technology industries. A version of media studies which describes what is still and for the foreseeable future the dominant media platform globally – television – as 'legacy' media, is the product of fashion rather than informed knowledge. The use of terms such as 'legacy' media or 'heritage' media is not at all helpful; they reveal an ignorance of media history as well as a poor understanding of how the media operates, and how it is consumed, around the globe right now. As any good student of media history knows, these trajectories are just not that simple. New media has *not* displaced television globally, for instance; South Korea has the highest percentage penetration for broadband worldwide, it sets the standard for internet speeds, but more than 90 per cent of its citizens have subscription television and 90 per cent *of them* use their subscription television to watch free-to-air television, which consequently still leads the ratings. In the UK, television viewing is on the increase again, standing at around 7,000 minutes per person per month. Against this, as Des Freedman puts it, consumers spent a 'mere 48 minutes per month on Facebook and a paltry 33 minutes per month using Twitter' (Freedman, 2015: 122). These are 2013 figures, but nonetheless, the differentials are telling and are repeated in many parts of the world.

Finally, I think there is truth in the perception that the alignment between elements of new media studies and the entrepreneurial values of cool capitalism has resulted in media studies relinquishing some of its traditional scepticism about the information it gleans from the media industries. This is a cause for concern. It would be regrettable if media studies was to withdraw any further from its fundamental commitment to subjecting the activities, interests and power of the media industries – old and new – to close, independent and critical scrutiny. While such work is certainly still going on, I acknowledge, there is a danger that it could become a casualty of digital optimism; I am not the only one who has argued in recent times that the field needs a renewed commitment to the analysis of media power (Curran, 2011; Fenton, 2013b). I want to suggest that the divided curriculum plays its part in this tendency. It is possible to see, crudely I admit, a contrast between the politics customarily underlying the approaches taken towards the traditional media, most of which are still interested in the protection of the public good, for instance, and those taken towards the new media, where there is comparatively less interest in and patience with such an orientation. Perhaps this is due to new media studies' closer alignment with the communitarian rhetoric and start-up ethos of so many new media enterprises; there is a greater tendency to behave as if the positive changes in the disposition of media power that the digital optimists predicted have already happened and the problems underpinning traditional media studies can now be consigned to the past. At the more extreme end of that spectrum of differences, however, we can also find within new media studies an unapologetic alignment with a ruggedly individualistic mode of entrepreneurial capitalism that would respond to the kind of issues raised about the media and privacy in this book, for instance, by telling me to just 'get over it, privacy is an outdated concept'.

These generalisations might not ring true for everyone and they are, as I say, drawn from my own experience rather than from a comprehensive survey of how these two fields have been articulated in various locations. But I think there is something to worry about here. The prospect that worries me most is that the divided curriculum has the potential over time to establish two very different models of the politics of media studies – importantly, with two different models of what *its point* would be – rather than merely a difference in the technologies upon which they focus. This would be a regrettable outcome of the divided curriculum, diminishing the critical purchase and intellectual coherence of both sides of the divide.

Unifying the divided curriculum

To move into a more positive and constructive mode, it might help if I outlined some of what I would see as possibilities for an ecumenical solution. What could a more inclusive media studies curriculum look like? For a start, I should say that it might not look radically different from what we tend to encounter now in terms of its actual content, but it would have significantly different intentions and therefore significantly different organising principles from many of the offerings currently in place. Its primary task, initially, would be to approach the media industries as a complex whole, bringing all these disparate platforms, formats and affordances together in an integrated account. My earlier suggestion that we might do this by outlining a continuum that takes us from the mass media through to the interpersonal affordances of connective media is one possible strategy of pulling together what is now a ramshackle assemblage of media theory into a more coherent and interrelated structure. The point of doing this would be to enable us to properly examine the media's social, political and cultural function. I am not suggesting that this would exclude the study of the structure of the media industries, or the understanding of media production; this would be just as necessary in the curriculum I am envisaging as it is for the current formations of the field. However, and forgive me if this seems terribly obvious, but it seems most useful to frame the study of the media, at the outset, in ways that make it very clear *why* we should see that as an important endeavour. In my view, the substantive answer to that is an academic rather than a vocational one. That is, while we may indeed prepare students for careers in the media, and while we may well teach in programmes that provide training in specific areas of media production, the purpose of the academic examination of the media is related to the media's fundamental social, political and cultural importance – and our need to understand its influence and power. Therefore, that is what I would want to help my students understand in (let's call it) Media Studies 101, and it would be embedded as a continuing rationale, providing coherence for their programmes of study in subsequent courses.

Such an orientation would necessarily break with a platform-specific approach, at least in its first-level courses, in order to follow the kind of strategy I have used in designing this book. That is, it would focus on the large-scale, cross-cutting and cross-platform issues that structure what happens right across the media continuum. While these are necessarily 'big picture' issues, they can still be taught with constant reference to specific instances, involving a pedagogic practice of highlighting the historical, cultural, economic and political contingencies that determine how each issue plays out within particular regional, national or local contexts. Initially, the programme could be organised around what might be thought of as a menu of broad questions which focus most fully on the function of the media. That menu would include much of what we have discussed in the preceding chapters: the transformation of the media manifold in the post-mass-media era; the shifting relations between the media, the market and the state; the rationales, purposes and possible futures for media regulation; the media's capacity to shape our cultures and its changing role in the production of our cultural and community identities; and the varying structure, make-up and use of the media industries along the media continuum. Underpinning all of these would be the dual objectives of critically understanding what the media does, how it works, and in whose interests, on the one hand, and how we make use of the media and to what effect, on the other.

As students move through the programme, they would benefit from encountering a stronger methodological focus than tends to be currently taught in most of the media studies programmes I have encountered in recent years. Certain approaches that were once routinely taught have all but disappeared, effectively reducing the capabilities of our students by providing them with fewer resources to draw on when framing their analysis. For example, I hold the view that media students need to understand the value of political economy as a means of describing the structure of the media industries. Interrelations that are difficult to track across the continuum of technological affordances, or across platforms and genres of content, do tend to stand out when they are connected to the corporations or interests that own and control them. We live in a world of highly concentrated media ownership, and this concentration is made most clearly visible through political economy; it is much less visible if we stay with a more medium-specific, platform-specific or format-specific approach. I am mindful, in making this comment, of Geert Lovink's (2013) recent call for a political economy of social media as a necessary way of understanding what has happened as it has mutated from an open field into a 'walled garden' – examining its commercial function, purpose and organisational structure rather than only investigating the ways in which consumers describe how they make use of it.

Earlier, I noted the need for a greater consideration of the continuities in the structure and function of the media over time; in this teaching programme, such a consideration would be particularly useful for understanding the complexities and consequences of the decline of the mass media paradigm. We can access that longer view, obviously, by paying more attention to media history – and not only the history of specific media (which does, understandably, tend to be a dominant way of teaching media history), but also of the broader relation between media technologies and society. There are a wide range of options to be taken up here: from communications theory (Castells, 2009), cultural histories of the media (Sconce, 2000; Spigel, 1992, 2001) or from the rich body of historicised theoretical work on the media industries that has developed out of the recent recovery of a focus on production (Holt and Perren, 2009). It would certainly be useful if the kinds of historical parallels I cited earlier from Michael Newman's history of video and James Curran's account of the fate of 'millenarian prophecy' were placed front and centre in media history classes so that students did not simply take the most recent signs for unique wonders.

It would also be useful if the transnationally comparative and interdisciplinary approaches that are now beginning to appear more often in the academic literatures in media and cultural studies also found their way into the teaching programme, as a way of underlining the local, cultural and historical specificity of media systems, the highly contingent take-up of media technologies, and their deeply located relation to the social. An interdisciplinary approach also has the capacity to transform the ways in which we talk about audiences and their practices of consumption, but there is still only limited exploration of that potential. That said, as a benefit of ethnographic work (and by this I mean long-term, fieldwork-based ethnography of the kind employed by cultural anthropology) that has focused on locations outside the Anglophone West (Straubhaar, 2007; Pertierra, 2009; Pertierra and Turner, 2013), we are beginning to develop a much richer, and more highly nuanced, understanding of what is involved in media consumption around the world. Importantly, the focus of such work is not particularly media-centric; rather, it is focused upon understanding how media practices of all kinds are variously integrated into the practices of everyday life, in these places, by these subjects, and at these times. The evidence of hybridisation that emerges from Madaniou and Miller's (2013) work, for instance, not only tells us about these audiences and the hybridity of their practices of media use, but also broadens our understanding of the practices of media use in general.

To bring this wish list to a close then, the concluding point I want to make is that only after bigger pictures such as these are established for the students, in my view, is it appropriate to then focus more narrowly on particular media, particular technologies, particular platforms, particular genres or particular formats. Ideally, this would be occurring at the upper levels of the undergraduate programme, and at that point, the distinctions and specificities which would emerge should have been sufficiently contextualised so that their character, function and implications could be properly assessed. It would also occur at a time when the programme had successfully instilled a clear sense of the dimensions and composition of the media manifold, in its totality. Most importantly, it would enable the more focused and platform-specific programmes of study to be framed within the larger understanding of the media's social function.

Conclusion

One of the presentations I made during the period I was planning this book contributed to the colloquium series at the Annenberg School for Communication at the University of Pennsylvania, where I had previously the privilege of being a guest of their Scholars' Program in Culture and Communication. In what was an extremely useful question period at the end of my presentation, Michael Delli Carpini asked me a question which went along the following lines. There are three standard narratives in critical accounts of contemporary media, he said. One tells us that despite all the volatility and publicity about transformative new technologies, actually very little has changed. The second tells us that *everything* has changed, that we are looking at an entirely new mediascape into the future, that the people have finally regained control over the media, and that from now on it's all going to be wonderful. And the third narrative also tells us that everything has changed but that this is entirely for the worst and 'we are all going to hell in a handbasket'. Given these three options, he asked, 'what's your narrative'? A good question, and one that I couldn't answer particularly well at the time, although I agreed that these did seem to be the standard options for large synoptic accounts of the contemporary state of the media or media studies.

Corner and Pels make a similar point on the standard options for an account such as this, but they only offer two narratives. The first is what they call the 'enabling' view of the media which is the traditional liberal-democratic view that has the media enabling democracy by informing the public and protecting their interests against other sources of power. The second, and as they say the far more familiar view these days, is the 'disabling' view which has the media 'variously undermining the practice of democracy or, at least, having a strong propensity to do so':

> They perform their subversive function through such routes as the substitution of entertainment for knowledge, the closing off of true diversity, the pursuit of an agenda determined primarily by market factors and their susceptibility to control by government and corporate agencies. (Corner and Pels, 2003: 4)

A great deal of what I have said in this book could fit into that second narrative, as most of these are concerns that I think have been exacerbated by the manner in which the media has re-invented itself. However, there is a crucial difference: I don't see the media as either 'enabling' or 'disabling'. That locates them definitively in a secondary role to other sources of power. Rather than characterising them in this way, I see the media as powerful in themselves. In some cases, the media are in fact a primary location of power; in most cases, they constitute a location of power that is, at the very least, devoted to serving their own interests. This doesn't mean that the media has to always or even necessarily work against the interests of the public, of those of democracy – in many cases, these interests are easily, if strategically rather than organically, aligned. But, the reconfiguration of media power outlined in so much of this book does reflect a significant change in the orientation of our media institutions and the media industries. Hence the need for renewed scrutiny from a discipline such as ours.

I don't quite make it into the 'to hell in a handbasket' scenario, then, but my task in this book is to respond to Michael Delli Carpini's challenge by coming up with a fourth narrative. This is how it goes: the media has re-invented itself, this has involved major changes and the social and political implications of these changes are varied but increasingly concerning. However, the current state of media studies is no longer fit for the purpose of properly understanding these changes, accurately assessing their implications, and then addressing these concerns. That needs to be fixed. By taking us back to some core, cross-cutting issues at the heart of the serious political and social issues we need to address in relation to the re-invented media, and by attempting to reintegrate the disaggregated approaches that have dominated the recent history of media studies into a more coherent and inclusive whole, I am hoping that this book will contribute to a renewal of media studies' fitness for purpose in the present conjuncture.

BIBLIOGRAPHY

Anderson, C. (2004) 'The long tail', *Wired* 12: 10. www.wired.com/wired/archive/12.10/tail.html.
Anderson, C. (2006) *The Long Tail: Why the Future of Business is Selling Less of More*, London: Hyperion.
Andrejevic, M. (2004) *Reality TV: The Work of Being Watched*, Lanham, MD: Rowman and Littlefield.
Andrejevic, M. (2007) *iSpy: Surveillance and Power in the Interactive Era*, Lawrence, Kansas: University Press of Kansas.
Andrejevic, M. (2013) *Infoglut: How Too Much Information Is Changing the Way We Think and Know*, New York: Routledge.
Appleyard, B. (2014) 'The long tail cut short: the economics of blockbuster capitalism', *New Statesman*, 16 January, 2014. www.newstatesman.com/2014/01/long-tail-cut-short-economics-blockbuster-capitalism. Accessed 18 January, 2014.
Athique, A.M. (2009) 'From monopoly to polyphony: India in the era of television' in G. Turner and J. Tay (eds) *Television Studies after TV: Understanding Television in the Post-Broadcast Era*, London and New York: Routledge, 159–167.
Banet-Weiser, S. (2012) *Authentic: The Politics of Ambivalence in a Brand Culture*, New York: New York University Press.
Baym, N. (2010) *Personal Connections in the Digital Age*, Cambridge: Polity.
Bednarski, P. (2015) 'That's the sway it is: young viewers trust YouTube stars most of all', *Online VideoDaily Video Blog*, March 5, www.mediapost.com/publications/article/245055/thats-the-sway-it-is-young-viewers-trust-youtube.html. Last accessed 11 March, 2015.
Bennett, J. (2011) *Television Personalities: Stardom and the Small Screen*, London and New York: Routledge.
Bennett, J. and Strange, N. (2015) (eds) *Media Independence: Working for Freedom or Working for Free?* New York and London: Routledge.
Bonner, F. (2003) *Ordinary Television: Analyzing Popular TV*, London: Sage.
Boorstin, D. (1971) *The Image: A Guide to Pseudo-Events in America*, New York: Atheneum.

Bourdieu, P. (1991) *Language and Symbolic Power*, Cambridge: Polity.
boyd, d. (2014) *It's Complicated: The Social Lives of Networked Teens*, New Haven and London: Yale University Press.
Boyle. R. and Kelly, L.W. (2010) 'The celebrity entrepreneur on television: profile, politics and power', *Celebrity Studies*, 1: 3, pp. 334–350.
Bratich, J. (2007) 'Programming reality: control societies, new subjects, powers of transformation', in D. Heller (ed.) *Makeover Television: Realities Remodelled*, London: I.B.Tauris.
Bruns, A. (2008) *Blogs, Wikipedia, Second Life, and Beyond: From Production to Produsage*, New York: Peter Lang.
Buonanno, M. (2008) *The Age of Television: Experiences and Theories*, trans. Jennifer Radice, Bristol: Intellect.
Castells, M. (2009) *Communication Power*, Oxford: Oxford University Press.
Chalaby, J. (2005) (ed.) *Transnational Television Worldwide: Towards a New Media Order*, London: I.B.Tauris.
Chua, B.H. (2005) 'Liberalization without democratization: Singapore in the next decade', in F. Loh and J. Ojendal (eds) *Southeast Asian Responses to Globalization: Restructuring Governance and Deepening Democracy*, Singapore: Institute of Southeast Asian Studies, 57–82.
Chua, B. H. (2011) 'Singapore as model: planning innovations, knowledge experts', in A. Roy and A. Ong (eds) *Worlding Cities: Asian Experiments and the Art of Being Global*, Malden, Oxford: Wiley-Blackwell, 29–53.
Collins, S. (2008) 'Making the most out of 15 minutes: reality TV's dispensable celebrity', *Television and New Media*, 9: 2, 87–110.
Corner, J. and Pels, D. (2003) (eds) *Media and the Restyling of Politics*, London: Sage.
Cottle, S. (2003) (ed.) *News, Public Relations and Power*, London: Sage.
Couldry, N. (2003) *Media Rituals: A Critical Approach*, London and New York: Routledge.
Couldry, N. (2012) *Media, Society, World: Social Theory and Digital Media Practice*, Cambridge: Polity.
Couldry, N., Livingstone, S. and Markham, T. (2007) 'Celebrity culture and public connection: bridge or chasm?', *International Journal of Cultural Studies*, 10: 4, 403–422.
Couldry, N., Livingstone, S., and Markham, T. (2010) *Media Consumption and Public Engagement: Beyond the Presumption of Intention*, London: Palgrave.
Couldry, N., Madaniou, M. and Pinchevski, A. (2013) (eds) *Ethics of Media*, London: Palgrave.
Cunningham, S. and Flew, T. (2002) 'Policy', in S. Cunningham and G. Turner (eds) *The Media and Communications in Australia*, St Leonards: Allen and Unwin.
Curran, J. (2010) 'The future of journalism', *Journalism Studies*, 11: 4, 464–476.
Curran, J. (2011) *Media and Democracy*, London and New York: Routledge.
Curran, J. (2012) 'Rethinking internet history', in J. Curran, N. Fenton and D. Freedman (eds) *Misunderstanding the Internet*, London: Routledge, 35–65.
Curran, J., Fenton, N. and Freedman, D. (2012) (eds) *Misunderstanding the Internet*, London: Routledge.
Curran, J. and Park, M. (2000) (eds) *De-Westernizing Media Studies*, Routledge: London.
Curtin, M. (2004) 'Media capitals', in L. Spigel and J. Olsen (eds) *Television after TV: Essays on a Medium in Transition*, Durham NC: Duke University Press, 270–302.
Curtin, M. (2007) *Playing to the World's Largest Audience: The Globalization of Chinese Film and TV*, Berkeley: University of California Press.
Dahlgren, P. (2009) *Media and Political Engagement: Citizens, Communication and Democracy*, Cambridge: Cambridge University Press.
Davies, N. (2014) *Hack Attack!: How the Truth Caught up with Rupert Murdoch*, London: Chatto and Windus.

Davis, A. (2003) 'Public relations and news sources', in S. Cottle (ed.) *News, Public Relations and Power*, London: Sage, 27–42.

Dayan, D. (2009) 'Sharing and showing: television as monstration', *Annals of the American Academy of Political and Social Science*, 625: 19–31.

Deloitte (2009) 'State of the media democracy 2009 survey', 7 January, www.deloitte.com/us/realitycheck. Accessed 30 January, 2009.

Deuze, M. (2007) *Media Work*, Cambridge: Polity.

Dhoest, A. (2013) 'The persistence of national TV: language and cultural proximity in Flemish fiction', in M. de Valck and J. Teurlings (eds) *After the Break: Television Theory Today*, Amsterdam: Amsterdam University Press, 51–64.

Driessens, O. (2013) 'The celebritization of society and culture: understanding the structural dynamics of celebrity culture', *International Journal of Cultural Studies*, 16: 6, 641–657.

Dyer, R. (1979) *Stars*, London: BFI.

Edwards, L. and Jeffries, E. (eds) (2010) *Celebrity in China*, Hong Kong: University of Hong Kong Press.

Elberse, A. (2014) *Blockbusters: Why Big Hits – and Big Risks – Are the Future of the Entertainment Business*, London: Faber and Faber.

Ellis, J. (2002) *Seeing Things: Television in the Age of Uncertainty*, London: I.B.Tauris.

Fenton, N. (2013a) 'The internet and social networking', in J. Curran, N. Fenton and D. Freedman (eds) *Misunderstanding the Internet*, London: Routledge, 123–148.

Fenton, N. (2013b) 'Cosmopolitanism as conformity and contestation', *Journalism Studies*, 5: 2, 172–186.

Flew, T. (2007) *New Media: An Introduction*, Oxford: Oxford University Press.

Flew, T., Iosifidis, P. and Steemers, J. (eds) (2015) *Global Media and National Policies: The Return of the State*, London: Palgrave.

Franklin, B. (1997) *Newszak and News Media*, London: Edward Arnold.

Franklin, B., Hogan, M., Langley, Q., Mosdell, N. and Pile, E. (2009) *Key Concepts in Public Relations*, London: Sage.

Freedman, D. (2006) 'Internet transformations: "old" media resilience in the "new media" revolution', in J. Curran and D. Morley (eds) *Media and Cultural Theory*, London and New York: Routledge, 275–290.

Freedman, D. (2015) 'The resilience of TV and its implications for media policy', in K. Oakley and J. O'Connor (eds) *The Routledge Companion to the Cultural Industries*, London and New York: Routledge, 120–129.

Gabler, N. (1995) *Walter Winchell: Gossip, Power and the Culture of Celebrity*, London: Picador.

Gamson, J. (1994) *Claims to Fame: Celebrity in Contemporary America*, Berkeley: University of California Press.

Garcia Canclini, N. (2014) *Imagined Globalization*, trans. G. Yudice, Durham, NC: Duke University Press.

Gauntlett, D. (2007) 'Media studies 2.0', Theory.org, 24 February, www.theory.org.uk/mediastudies2.htm.

Gerson, I. (2010) *The Breakup 2.0*, Ithaca, NY: Cornell University Press.

Goggin, G. and Hjorth, L. (2009) (eds) *Mobile Technologies: From Telecommunications to New Media*, New York: Routledge.

Goskilo, H. and Strukov, V. (2011) (eds) *Celebrity and Glamour in Contemporary Russia: Shocking Chic*, London: Routledge.

Grindstaff, L. (2014) 'DI(t)Y, reality-style: the cultural work of ordinary celebrity', in L. Ouellette (ed.) *The Companion to Reality Television*, Boston: Wiley, 234–344.

Hall, S. (1982) 'The rediscovery of "ideology": the return of the "repressed" in media studies', in M. Gurevitch, T. Bennett, J. Curran and J. Woollacott (eds) *Culture, Media and Society*, London: Methuen, 56–90.
Hallin, D. and Mancini, P. (2004) *Comparing Media Systems: Three Models of Media and Politics*, New York: Cambridge University Press.
Hartley, J. (1992) *The Politics of Pictures: The Creation of the Public in the Age of Popular Media*, London: Routledge.
Hartley, J. (1999) *Uses of Television*, London and New York: Routledge.
Havens, T., Lotz, A., and Tinic, S. (2009) 'Critical media industry studies: a research approach', *Communication, Culture and Critique*, 2, 234–253.
Havens, T. and Lotz, A. (2011) *Understanding Media Industries*, New York: Oxford University Press.
Hay, J. and Ouelette, L. (2008) *Better Living through Reality TV: Television and Post-Welfare Citizenship*, Malden, MA: Blackwell.
Hepp, A. (2013) *Cultures of Mediatization*, London: Polity.
Hermes, J. (2013) 'Caught: critical versus everyday perspectives on television', in M. de Valck and J. Teurlings (eds) *After the Break: Television Theory Today*, Amsterdam: Amsterdam University Press, 35–49.
Hillis, J., Petit, M., and Jarrett, J. (2013) *Google and the Culture of Search*, London and New York: Routledge.
Hindman, M. (2009) *The Myth of Digital Democracy*. Princeton and Oxford: Princeton University Press.
Hjarvard, S. (2013) *The Mediatization of Culture and Society*, London and New York: Routledge.
Holmes, S. and Redmond, S. (2006) (eds) *Framing Celebrity: New Directions in Celebrity Culture*, London: Routledge.
Holt, J. and Perren, A. (2009) *Media Industries: History, Theory, Method*, Malden, MA: Wiley-Blackwell.
Holt, J. and Sanson, K. (2014) (eds) *Connected Viewing: Selling, Streaming, and Sharing Media in the Digital Era*, London and New York: Routledge.
Howley, K. (2013) (ed.) *Media Interventions*, New York: Peter Lang.
Inglis, F. (2010) *A Short History of Celebrity*, Princeton and Oxford: Princeton University Press.
Inhorn, S. and Street, J. (2011) 'Simon Cowell for Prime Minister? Young citizens' attitudes towards celebrity politics', *Media, Culture and Society*, 33: 3, 1–11.
Isaacson, W. (2013) *Steve Jobs*, New York: Simon and Schuster.
Jenkins, H. (1992) *Textual Poachers: Television Fans and Participatory Culture*, New York: Routledge.
Jenkins, H. (2006) *Convergence Culture: Where Old and New Media Collide*, New York and London: New York University Press.
Jericho, G. (2012) *The Rise of the Fifth Estate: Social Media and Blogging in Australian Politics*, Melbourne: Scribe.
Kaneva, N. (2012) (ed.) *Branding Post-Communist Nations: Marketizing National Identities in the 'New' Europe*, London and New York: Routledge.
Katz, E. and Scannell, P. (eds) 'The end of television? Its impact on the world (so far)', special issue of *The Annals of the American Academy of Political and Social Science*, 625: 6.
Keane, M., Fung, A. and Moran, A. (2007) *New Television: Globalisation and the East Asian Cultural Imagination*, Hong Kong: Hong Kong University Press.
Khorana, S. (2012) 'English-language television news and the great Indian middle class: made for each other?', *Studies in South Asian Film and Media*, 4: 1, April.

Khorana, S. (2014) 'The political is populist: talk shows, political debates, and the middle-class public sphere in India', *Media International Australia*, 152, August, 98–118.

Khorana, S., Parthasarathi, V. and Thomas, P. (2014) (eds) 'Public spheres and the media in India', special issue of *Media International Australia*, 152.

Kraidy, M. (2010) *Reality Television and Arab Politics: Contention in Public Life*, New York: Cambridge University Press.

Kraidy, M. (2014) 'Mapping Arab television: structures, sites, genres, flows and politics', in K. Wilkins, J. Straubhaar and S. Kumar (eds) *Global Communication*, New York: Routledge, 35–49.

Lee, H.J. and Andrejevic, M. (2014) 'Second screen theory: from the democratic surround to the digital enclosure' in J. Holt and K. Sanson (eds) *Connected Viewing: Selling, Streaming, and Sharing Media in the Digital Era*, London and New York: Routledge, 40–61.

Lewis, T. (2014) 'Life coaches, style mavens, and design gurus: everyday experts on reality television', in L. Ouellette (ed.) *The Companion to Reality Television*, Boston: Wiley, 402–420.

Littler, J. (2007) 'Celebrity CEOs and the cultural economy of tabloid intimacy', in S. Redmond and S. Holmes (eds) *Stardom and Celebrity: A Reader*, London: Sage.

Livingstone, S. (2009) 'On the mediation of everything: ICA presidential address, 2008', *Journal of Communication*, 59: 1, 1–18.

Lotz, A. (2014a) *The Television Will Be Revolutionized*, London and New York: New York University Press, second edition. First edition published 2007.

Lotz, A. (2014b) *Cable Guys: Television and Masculinities in the 21st Century*, New York and London: New York University Press.

Lovink, G. (2008) *Zero Comments: Blogging and Critical Internet Culture*. New York and London: Routledge.

Lovink, G. (2013) 'A world beyond Facebook: introduction to the *Unlike Us Reader*', in G. Lovink and M. Rasch (eds) *Unlike Us: Social Media Monopolies and Their Alternatives*, Amsterdam: Institute of Network Cultures, 9–16.

Lovink, G. and Rasch, M. (2013) (eds) *Unlike Us: Social Media Monopolies and Their Alternatives*, Amsterdam: Institute of Network Cultures.

Ma, E. (2012) *Desiring Hong Kong, Consuming South China: Transborder Cultural Politics 1970–2010*, Hong Kong: Hong Kong University Press.

McChesney, R.W. (2007) *Communication Revolution: Critical Junctures and the Future of Media*, New York and London: The New Press.

McCutcheon, L., Maltby, J., Houran, J. and Ashe, D. (2004) *Celebrity Worshippers: Inside the Minds of Stargazers*, Baltimore, MD: PublishAmerica.

McGuigan, J. (2000) 'British identity and the "People's Princess"', *The Sociological Review*, February, 1: 48, 1–18.

McGuigan, J. (2006) 'The politics of cultural studies and cool capitalism', *Cultural Politics*, 2: 2, 137–158.

McGuigan, J. (2009) *Cool Capitalism*, London: Pluto.

McNamara, K. (2011) 'The paparazzi industry and new media: the evolving production and consumption of celebrity news and gossip', *International Journal of Cultural Studies*, 14: 5, 515–530.

Madaniou, M. (2013) 'Ethics of mediation and the voice of the injured subject' in N. Couldry, M. Madaniou and A. Pinchevski (2013) (eds) *Ethics of Media*, London: Palgrave, 178–197.

Madaniou, M. and Miller, D. (2013) 'Polymedia: towards a new theory of digital media in interpersonal communication', *International Journal of Cultural Studies*, 16: 2, 169–187.

Maliki, J. (2008) 'Cultural identity and cultural representations on reality TV: an analysis of *Akademi Fantasia*', unpublished MA thesis, University of Queensland, Australia.

Manovich, L. (2008) 'The practice of everyday (media) life', in G. Lovink and S. Niederer (eds) *Video Vortex: Responses to YouTube*, Amsterdam: Institute of Network Cultures, 33–44.

Marshall, P.D. (1997) *Celebrity and Power: Fame in Contemporary Culture*, Minneapolis and London: University of Minnesota Press.

Marshall, P.D. (2006) 'New media – new self: the changing power of celebrity' in P.D. Marshall (ed.) *The Celebrity Culture Reader*, London and New York: Routledge, 634–644.

Marshall, P.D. (2010) 'The promotion and presentation of the self: celebrity as a marker of presentational media', *Celebrity Studies*, 1: 1, 35–48.

Martell, L. (2007) 'The third wave in globalization theory', *International Studies Review*, 9: 173–196.

Marwick, A.E. (2013) *Status Update: Celebrity, Publicity, and Branding in the Social Media Age*, New Haven and London: Yale University Press.

Marwick, A. and boyd, d. (2011) 'To see and be seen: celebrity practice on Twitter', *Convergence*, 17: 2, 139–158.

Meikle, G. and Young, S. (2012) *Media Convergence: Networked Digital Media in Everyday Life*, London: Palgrave Macmillan.

Mihelj, S. (2011) *Media Nations: Communication, Belonging and Exclusion in the Modern World*, London: Palgrave Macmillan.

Mohammed, D. (2012), 'Popular music, reality television and the cultural identity of the urban poor in Dhaka', unpublished PhD thesis, University of Queensland, Australia.

Morley, D. (2007) *Media, Modernity and Technology: The Geography of the New*, London and New York: Routledge.

Mortensen, M. and Jerslev, A. (2014) 'Taking the extra out of the extraordinary: paparazzi photography as an online celebrity news genre', *International Journal of Cultural Studies*, 17: 6, 619–636.

Napoli, P. (2008) 'Hyperlinking and the forces of "massification"', in J. Turow and L. Tsui (eds) *The Hyperlinked Society*, Ann Arbor: University of Michigan Press, 56–69.

Negroponte, N. (1995) *Being Digital*, New York: Alfred Knopf.

Newman, M.Z. (2014) *Video Revolutions: On the History of a Medium*, New York: Columbia University Press.

Ong, J. (2015) 'The television of intervention: mediating patron–client ties in the Philippines', in J. Tay and G. Turner (eds) *Television Histories in Asia*, London: Routledge, 144–163.

Oren, T. (2012) 'Reiterational texts and global imagination: television strikes back', in T. Oren and S. Shahaf (eds) *Global Television Formats: Understanding Television across Borders*, New York and London: Routledge, 366–381.

Oren, T. and Shahaf, S. (2012) (eds) *Global Television Formats: Understanding Television across Borders*, New York and London: Routledge.

Ouellette, L. (2014) (ed.) *A Companion to Reality Television*, Boston: Wiley.

Pertierra, A.C. (2009) 'Private pleasures: watching videos in post-Soviet Cuba', *International Journal of Cultural Studies*, 12: 2, 113–130.

Pertierra, A.C. and Turner, G. (2013) *Locating Television: Zones of Consumption*, London and New York: Routledge.

Phillips, A. (2013) 'Journalism, ethics and the impact of competition', in Couldry, N., Madaniou, M. and Pinchevski, A. (eds) *Ethics of Media*, London: Palgrave, 255–270.

Potter, J.A. (2013) 'The expanding role for media literacy in the age of participatory cultures', in A. Delwiche and J.J. Henderson (eds) *The Participatory Cultures Handbook*, New York and London: Routledge, 232–243.

Rein, I., Kotler, P. and Stoller, M. (1997) *High Visibility: The Making and Marketing of Professionals and Celebrities*, Lincolnwood, IL: NTC Business Books.

Riegert, K. (2009) (ed.) *Politicotainment: Television's Take on the Real*, New York: Peter Lang.

Rojek, C. (2001) *Celebrity*, London: Reaktion.

Rojek, C. (2012) *Fame Attack: The Inflation of Celebrity and Its Consequences*, London: Bloomsbury.

Rosen, J. (2006) 'The people formerly known as the audience', PressThink: Ghost of Democracy in the Media Machine, 27 June, http://journalism.nyu.ed/pubzon3e/weblogs/pressthinkg/2006/06/27ppl_frmer.html. Last accessed 25 November, 2008.

Ross, S.M. (2008) *Beyond the Box: Television and the Internet*, Malden, MA: Blackwell.

Rowe, D. (2015) 'Online tabloid newspapers', in T. Miller (ed.) *Routledge Companion to Global Popular Culture*, New York: Routledge, 323–332.

Ruddock, A. (2013) *Youth and Media*, London: Sage.

Sakr, N. (2007) *Arab Television Today*, London: I.B.Tauris.

Schwichtenberg, C. (1992) (ed.) *The Madonna Connection: Representational Politics, Subcultural Identities and Cultural Theory*, Boulder, CO: Westview Press.

Sconce, J. (2000) *Haunted Media: Electronic Presence from Telegraphy to Television*, Durham, NC: Duke University Press.

Sender, K. (2012) *The Makeover: Reality Television and Reflexive Audiences*, New York: New York University Press.

Senft, T. (2008) *Camgirls: Celebrity and Community in the Age of Social Media*, New York: Peter Lang.

Skeggs, B. and Wood, H. (2012) *Reacting to Reality Television: Performance, Audience and Value*, London: Routledge.

Spigel, L. (1992) *Make Room for TV: Television and the Family Ideal in Postwar America*, Chicago: University of Chicago Press.

Spigel, L. (2001) *Welcome to the Dreamhouse: Popular Media and Postwar Suburbs*, Durham, NC: Duke University Press.

Straubhaar, J. (2007) *World Television: From Global to Local*, Thousand Oaks, CA: Sage.

Straubhaar, J. (2014) 'Mapping "global" in global communication and media studies', in K. Wilkins, J. Straubhaar and S. Kumar (eds) *Global Communication*, New York: Routledge, 10–34.

Sudhaman, A. (2014) 'Global PR industries growth surges to 11% in 2013'. *Holmes Report: World PR Report*. www.worldreport.holmesresport.com. Accessed 12 January, 2015.

Sun, W. and Zhao, Y. (2009) 'Television culture with "Chinese characteristics": the politics of compassion and education', in G. Turner and J. Tay (eds) *Television Studies after TV: Understanding Television in the Post-broadcast Era*, London: Routledge, 96–104.

Sunstein, C. (2009) *Republic.com 2.0*, Princeton: Princeton University Press.

Taylor, A. (2011) *Single Women in Popular Culture: The Limits of Postfeminism*, London: Palgrave.

Terranova, T. (2000) 'Free labor: producing culture for the digital economy', *Social Text*, 18: 2, 33–58.

Thompson, J. (1995) *The Media and Modernity*. Cambridge: Polity.

Tinic, S. (2005) *On Location: Canada's Television Industry in a Global Market*, Toronto: University of Toronto Press.

Turner, G. (2009) 'Television and the nation: does this matter any more?', in G. Turner and J. Tay (eds) *Television Studies after TV: Understanding Television in the Post-broadcast Era*, London and New York: Routledge, 54–64

Turner, G. (2010) *Ordinary People and the Media: The Demotic Turn*, London: Sage.

Turner, G. (2011a) 'Convergence and divergence: the international experience of digital television', in J. Bennett and N. Strange (eds) *Television as Digital Media*, Durham, NC and London: Duke University Press, 31–51.

Turner, G. (2011b) 'Surrendering the space: convergence culture, cultural studies, and the curriculum', *Cultural Studies* 25: 4–5, 685–699.
Turner, G. (2014a) 'Is celebrity news, news?', *Journalism: Theory, Practice and Criticism*, 15: 2, 144–152.
Turner, G. (2014b) *Understanding Celebrity*, London: Sage, revised edition.
Turner, G. (2015) 'Celebrity, participation and the public', in P.D. Marshall and S. Redmond (eds) *The Oxford Companion to Celebrity Culture*, in press.
Turner, G., Bonner, F. and Marshall, P.D. (2000) *Fame Games: The Production of Celebrity in Australia*, Melbourne: Cambridge University Press.
Turner, G. and Cunningham, S. (2002) 'The media and communications in Australia today', in S. Cunningham and G. Turner (eds) *The Media and Communications in Australia*, St Leonards: Allen and Unwin.
Turner, G. and Tay, J. (2009) (eds) *Television Studies after TV: Understanding Television in the Post-broadcast Era*, London and New York: Routledge.
Turow, J. (2011) *The Daily You: How the New Advertising Industry Is Defining Your Identity and Your Worth*, New Haven and London: Yale University Press.
Tussey, E. (2014) 'Connected viewing on the second screen: the limitations of the living room', in J. Holt and K. Sanson (eds) *Connected Viewing: Selling, Streaming, and Sharing Media in the Digital Era*, London and New York: Routledge, 202–216.
van Dijck, J. (2013) *The Culture of Connectivity: A Critical History of Social Media*, Oxford: Oxford University Press.
van Krieken, R. (2012) *Celebrity Society*, London: Routledge.
Volcic, Z. (2009) 'Television in the Balkans: the rise of commercial nationalism', in G. Turner and J. Tay (eds) *Television Studies after TV: Understanding Television in the Post-broadcast Era*, London and New York: Routledge, 115–124.
Volcic, Z. (2011) *Serbian Spaces of Identity: Narratives of Belonging by the Last 'Yugo' Generation*, New York: Hampton Press.
Volcic, Z. (2013) 'Commercial and sexualised nationalism on Serbian TV', *International Journal of Cultural Studies*, 16: 6, 597–614.
Volcic, Z. and Andrejevic, M. (2011) 'Nation branding in the era of commercial nationalism', *International Journal of Communications*, 5: 598–618.
Volcic, Z. and Andrejevic, M. (forthcoming) (eds) *Commercial Nationalism*, London: Palgrave Macmillan.
Voltmer, K. (2013) *The Media in Transitional Democracies*, Cambridge: Polity.
Warner, B. (2014) 'The 25 highest earning YouTube stars', *Celebrity Networth*, www.celebritynetworth.com/articles/celebrity/the-25-highest-earning-youtube-stars. Accessed January 12, 2015.
Weber, B. (2009) *Makeover TV: Selfhood, Citizenship and Celebrity*, Durham, NC: Duke University Press.
Weber, B. (2014) 'Mapping the makeover maze: The contours and contradictions of makeover television', in L. Ouelette (ed.) *A Companion to Reality Television*, Malden, MA: Wiley-Blackwell, 369–385.
Wernick, A. (1991) *Promotional Culture: Advertising, Ideology and Symbolic Expression*, London: Sage.
Whannel, G. (2002) *Media Sports Stars: Masculinities and Moralities*, London and New York: Routledge.
Wheeler, M. (2013) *Celebrity Politics*, London: Polity.
Wilkins, K.G. (2014) 'Mobilizing global communication: for what and for whom?', in K.G. Wilkins, J. Straubhaar and S. Kumar (eds) *Global Communication*, New York: Routledge, 100–118.

Wilkins, K.G., Straubhaar, J. and Kumar, S. (2014) (eds) *Global Communication*, New York: Routledge.

Wilkins, K.G., Straubhaar, J. and Kumar, S. (2014) 'Introduction: new agendas in global communication', in K.G. Wilkins, J. Straubhaar and S. Kumar (eds) *Global Communication*, New York: Routledge, 1–9.

Wilson, J.A. (2014) 'Reality television celebrity: star consumption and self-production in media culture', in L. Ouelette (ed.) *A Companion to Celebrity Culture*, Malden, MA: Wiley-Blackwell, 421–436.

Yudice, G. (2014) 'Translator's introduction', in N. Garcia Canclini, *Imagined Globalization*, trans. G. Yudice, Durham, NC: Duke University Press.

Zelizer, B. (2015) 'Terms of choice: uncertainty, journalism and crisis', *Journal of Communication*, forthcoming.

INDEX

Akademi Fantasia 71–2
Anderson, C. 25, 26
Appleyard, B. 26
Andrejevic, M. 3, 7, 22, 27, 28, 46–7, 50, 55, 78, 79, 80, 82, 90n, 110, 114, 117
Athique, A.M. 66

Banet-Weiser, S. 20, 22, 26–7, 54, 114, 120, 121
Baym, N. 23
Beck, U. 61
Bednarski, P. 112, 117
Bennett, J. 11
Bennett, J. and Strange, N. 75
Bernays, E. 108
Beyond the Box 54–5
Bonner, F. 93, 109
Boorstin, D. 97
Bourdieu, P. 34
Boyle, R. and Kelly, L.W. 94
Bratich, J. 14, 116, 123
Bruns, A. 21, 22
Bunting, S. 54–5
Buonanno, M. 6

Cable Guys 41
Castells, M. 6, 134
celebrity:
culture, rise of 11–12; 108–111, 120–123;
news 95–9; and the image 99–103; and gossip 103–5; and the paparazzi 99–102
online 120–2

Celebrity Society 121
Chalaby, J. 61
Chua, B.H. 65
Collins, S. 113
commercialisation 32–5, 128
Comparing Media Systems 45
consumption studies 29–30
convergence 24–28
Convergence Culture 25–6
Corner, J. and Pels, D. 94, 109, 135
Cottle, S. 97, 98
Couldry, N. 1, 3, 5, 6, 11, 23, 30, 31, 32, 34, 35, 39, 41, 112, 113, 123
Couldry, N, Livingstone, S. and Markham, T. 19, 105
Couldry, N., Madianou, M. and Pinchevski, A. 84
crisis in journalism 2, 7, 42–7, 81–4
Cunningham, S. and Flew, T. 24
Cunningham, S. and Turner, G. 24
Curran, J. 2, 7, 9, 39, 41, 42–3, 44, 45, 76, 81, 95, 130, 131
Curran, J. and Park, M. 59, 127
Curtin, M. 63, 127

Dahlgren, P. 39, 40, 65, 81
Daily You, The 20, 33, 52–3
Davies. N. 43–4
Davis, A. 97, 98
Dayan, D. 8, 61, 72, 103
Delli Carpini, M. 135
Deloitte 39
Deuze, M. 25, 81–2
Dhoest, A. 63

van Dijck. J. 3, 21–2, 31–2, 33–4, 56n, 61, 79, 125–6
Driessens, O. 94, 121–3 passim
Dyer, R. 108

Edwards, L. and Jeffries, E. 119
Elberse, A. 26
Ellis, J. 6, 50
entertainment, the rise of 38–46 passim
Ethics of Media 84

Fame Attack 108, 112
Fenton, N. 40, 45, 83, 88, 131
Flew, T. 60, 79–80
Flew, T. *et al.* 60
Franklin, B. 98
Franklin, B. *et al.* 9
Freedman, D. 8, 34, 63, 76, 130

Gabler, N. 103
Gamson, J. 107n, 110
Garcia Canclini, N. 68–9, 70
Gauntlett, D. 129
Gerson, I. 28
Global Communication 70
globalization and the media 67–72
Goggin, G. and Hjorth. L. 3
Google 47–50
Grindstaff, L. 112

Hallin, D. and Mancini, P. 45, 85
Hartley, J. 97, 98, 99, 114
Havens, T. *et al.* 41
Hay, J. and Ouelette, L. 114
Hepp, A. 25, 30, 31
Hermes, J. 6
Hillis, J. *et al.* 5, 40, 47, 49–50
Hindman, M. 26, 48, 61
Hjarvard, S. 30–31, 32, 33
Holmes, S. and Redmond, S. 110
Holt, J. and Perren, A. 134
Holt, J. and Sanson, K. 27

Imagined Globalization 69
Infoglut 51–2
information: commodification of 47–53; and the culture of search 47–53; decline of 38–41
Inglis, F. 100
Isaacson, W. 5

Jenkins, H. 6, 25–6, 60, 61

Kaneva, N. 9, 60, 67, 127
Katz, E. and Scannell, P. 60

Keane. M. *et al.* 119
Khorana, S. 7, 63, 67
Khorana, S. *et al.* 63
Kraidy, M. 2, 11, 41, 62, 71, 119
van Krieken, 94, 111, 119, 121
Kumar, S. 67

Lee, H.J. and Andrejevic, M. 51
Lewis, T. 109
Littler, J. 94
Livingstone, S. 30
Locating Television, 37n, 63
Lotz, A. 6, 41, 63
Lovink, G. 21, 26, 27, 34, 48, 52, 61, 133
Lovink, G. and Rasch, M. 21

Ma, E. 72
Madaniou, M. 35, 82–3, 88
Madaniou, M. and Miller, D. 3, 28, 29–30, 126, 134
McChesney, R. 2, 27, 81, 82, 105
McCutcheon, L. *et al.* 110
McGuigan, J. 4, 80, 110
McNamara, K. 100–102 passim
Maliki, J. 71, 119
Manovich, L. 51
Marshall, P.D. 11, 14, 101, 102, 109
Martell, L. 69
Marwick, A. 4, 5, 23, 25, 28, 37n, 93–4, 120–2 passim
Marwick, A. and boyd, d. 22
mass media paradigm, decline of 6–8, 19–24
Media and Democracy, The 39
Media Convergence 25
Media Nations 62
media power 32–36, 53–6, 127–128
media regulation and democracy 85–9
media-state relations 8–10; 60–7
media studies 126–8; and the divided curriculum 129–35
mediatization 30–2
Meikle, G. and Young, S. 25, 26, 63, 75, 76, 79, 81
Milhelj, S. 2, 9, 60, 61, 62, 67, 68, 71, 73, 85, 86
modernity and the media 60–7
Mohammed, D. 119
Morley, D. 29, 49, 61
Mortensen, M. and Jerslev, A. 99–100

Negroponte, N. 53
Newman, M. 23, 24, 26

Ong, J. 10
ordinary celebrity, the 111–113; and reality TV 113–120; online 120–2
Ordinary People and the Media 39, 71, 111
Oren, T. 61, 62

paparazzi 99–102
PewDiePie 93
Pertierra, A.C. 8, 37n, 63, 134
Pertierra, A.C. and Turner, G. 2, 8, 9, 28, 63, 65–6, 72, 73n, 134
Phillips, A. 83–4
privacy online 78–85
public good, the 32–6; and journalism 81–84; and the news 42–7
public relations 97–9

Reacting to Reality TV 115–116
Riegert, K. 94
Rojek, C. 11, 98, 108, 109, 112, 128
Rosen, J. 20, 21, 48, 128
Ross, S. 54
Rowe, D. 113

Sakr, N. 119
Schwichtenberg, C. 110
Sconce, J. 134
Sender, K. 110, 114, 117
Senft, T. 27, 110, 111
Skeggs, B. and Wood, H. 114–16
Spigel, L. 134
Stars 109
Status Update 93–4
Straubhaar, J. 62, 70, 127, 134
Sudhaman, A. 98
Sun, W. 88
Sun, W. and Zhao, Y. 2, 8
Sunstein, C. 6, 46, 52, 79, 128

Tay, J. 8, 63
Taylor, A. 117
television and the nation-state 60–7
Television Studies after TV 63
Television will be Revolutionized, The 63
Terranova, T. 22
Textual Poachers, 25
Thompson, J. 34
Tinic, S. 127
TMZ 93, 102
Turner, G. 2, 4, 5, 8, 19, 20, 26, 27, 39, 48, 71, 93, 105, 111, 117
Turner, G., Bonner, F. and Marshall, P.D. 98
Turner, G. and Tay, J. 8, 28, 63
Turow, J. 3, 20, 27, 33, 35–6, 52–3, 79
Tussey, E. 51

Understanding Celebrity 98

Volcic, Z. 34, 67
Volcic, Z. and Andrejevic, M. 10, 127
Voltmer, K. 2, 9, 10, 60, 62, 66, 76, 77, 85, 86–8, 89

Weber, B. 117–18
Wernick, A. 98
Whannel, G. 123n
Wife Swap 116–17
Wilkins, K.G., Straubhaar, J. and Kumar, S. 2, 70
Wilson, J. 109

Yudice, G. 69

Zelizer, B. 82